S0-BKA-021

141239

A GUIDE TO
HOMESCHOOLING FOR LIBRARIANS

A GUIDE TO
HOMESCHOOLING FOR
LIBRARIANS

BY DAVID C. BROSTROM

Highsmith
PRESS

Fort Atkinson, Wisconsin

Published by Highsmith Press
W5527 Highway 106
P.O. Box 800
Fort Atkinson, Wisconsin 53538-0800

1-800-558-2110

© David C. Brostrom, 1995.

Cover art by Mary Ann Highsmith

All rights reserved. Printed in the United States of America.
Except as permitted under the United States Copyright Act of 1976, no part of
this publication may be reproduced or distributed in any form or by any means,
or stored in a database or retrieval system, without the prior written permission
of the publisher.

The paper used in this publication meets the minimum requirements of
American National Standard for Information Science —
Permanence of Paper for Printed Library Material.
ANSI/NISO Z39.48-1992.

Library of Congress Cataloging-in-Publication Data

Brostrom, David C.
    A guide to homeschooling for librarians / by David C. Brostrom.
        p.   cm. -- (Highsmith Press handbook series)
    Includes bibliographical references and index.
    ISBN 0-917846-46-X (pbk. : alk. paper)
    1. Libraries and education--United States. 2. Homeschooling--
    United States I. Title. II. Series.
Z711.92.F34B76 1995
026.649'68--dc20   95-17056
                                                        CIP

ISBN 0·917846-46-X

26.64968
794g

L. I F. E Bible College
LIBRARY
1100 COVINA BLVD
SAN DIMAS, CA 91773

Contents

041468

L I F E Bible College
LIBRARY
1100 COVINA Blvd.
SAN DIMAS, CA 91773

041468

Foreword

When I started work at John Holt Associates in 1981, there were states where homeschooling was still illegal. In fact, one of my early jobs was to process a special stack of subscriptions marked "Brown Paper Wrapper," because these subscribers didn't want postal officials to know they were reading a publication with the title *Growing Without Schooling*. Now homeschooling is not only legal in all 50 states, but it has grown to become an eclectic, independent, and constantly increasing population of over 600,000 children today. The growth of homeschooling in America and throughout the world over the past two decades is changing our perceptions about what children can do and where they should be doing it during "school hours." It is creating new opportunities for people to share and develop their learning that go far beyond the "read a book and take a test" school curriculum most of us experienced as students.

Most public institutions that have contact with homeschoolers have been passively neutral or slow to respond positively to the growth of homeschooling and as a result they have lost some homeschoolers' confidence and support. But public libraries have been relatively quick to recognize and support their card-carrying members who do not send their children to school. By identifying and supporting homeschoolers as a clientele, libraries have also discovered a new source for active supporters and volunteers.

This book by David Brostrom will help any librarian wondering, "Who are these homeschoolers and what do they want from me and the library?" It will also serve as a sort of map that charts new land for learning opportunities that librarians, parents and communities can use. Libraries are not just communal book repositories but, as Mr. Brostrom makes clear, libraries are also non-compulsory centers for learning containing a wide variety of educational materials and experiences that benefit everyone in the community, not just homeschoolers. However, the most vital library resource is a knowledgeable and helpful librarian, and this short and wise book by Mr. Brostrom makes it clear how any librarian, regardless of their budget, can learn to serve homeschoolers.

By actively working with the homeschooling population, librarians also have the chance to let homeschoolers learn about the issues, concerns, and details that affect their library decisions, thereby nurturing a more informed, and one hopes a more supportive patron. In an age of tight funding and increased public skepticism about institutions, libraries and home-schoolers are creating new possibilities for learning in our communities. This book is a terrific guide for developing the public library's role in our fast-changing educational landscape.

PATRICK FARENGA, PUBLISHER
Growing Without Schooling
©1995 by Patrick Farenga

Preface

Someone once asked me why a librarian would want to write a book about home-schooling. I gave them a truthful answer. When I was a bookseller my business partners enthusiastically homeschooled their two children. Hannah and Rory went to school every day; at the bookstore we owned, at the karate gym, at a cooperative country school in the woods, and certainly at and around home. Nothing they did was traditional or mundane. They didn't seem to need a daily curriculum.

Other homeschooling parents I met were extremely loyal to what many people felt was a puzzling experiment with little potential for success. This divergence of opinions sparked my curiosity and I began to wonder what impact the movement would have on libraries. I had a hunch the number of home educators in the mid 1980s would double or triple by the mid 1990s. This meant a wide array of homeschoolers might make libraries, especially public libraries, their "home away from home," or as I like to call it—their laboratory. I also knew I was about to become involved in some capacity.

Statistics available at the time (1985) were just beginning to confirm my feelings. For a variety of reasons, many more people were choosing to teach their children at home. Small isolated pockets of home educator parents were beginning to form cohesive, politically active support groups. The popular media was taking notice. *In the years since 1985, the upsurge in home-schooling numbers has been more dramatic than expected.* Many states report a fivefold or even tenfold increase in the past decade. The word "momentum" comes to mind. Most importantly, at least from my inquiring professional perspective, as I checked around with colleagues, I realized that homeschooler usage of libraries was increasing significantly!

Because of the burgeoning number of homeschoolers using libraries, do we need to begin asking ourselves some important questions? What are my professional and personal feelings about homeschooling? How do I reach out and link up with the homeschooling community? What could I do once I'm linked up? Why would I want to get actively involved? How can I or others on our staff improve services to home educators? What are issues and problems that may surface? What about homeschool curricula in libraries? Who do I approach in the public schools with curriculum questions? How do I start a homeschool resource file? Finally, what is an effective, high quality service level to aim for?

A Guide To Homeschooling for Librarians is intended to answer your questions about:

- Types and styles of homeschoolers,

- What motivates homeschoolers,

- Tapping into your homeschool community,

- Time tested library programs and services,

- Challenges of serving home educators,

- Real-life experiences with home-schoolers,

- Distinctive homeschooling resources,

- How libraries can cooperate with public schools and homeschoolers,

- What impact home educators will have on libraries in the 1990s and beyond.

Two points of clarification: 1) When I use the word homeschoolers it refers to the parents who teach their children at home, the kids being taught, and the organized community of home educators; 2) there are two commonly accepted versions of the word(s) homeschooling; home schooling is the second choice. I tend to habitually use the first option.

1

Why All This Commotion about Homeschooling? An Overview of the Movement

In this country, and around the world, homeschooling has been practiced for centuries. It flourished during American colonial times, when parents commonly used a combination of tutors, apprenticeships and home teaching techniques. Many notable historical figures were schooled wholly or partially at home, including:

John Quincy Adams, Ben Franklin, Woodrow Wilson, Sally Ride, Franklin Roosevelt, Pearl Buck, Patrick Henry, Douglas MacArthur, George Washington, Agatha Christie, James Madison, Justice Sandra Day O'Connor, Abraham Lincoln, Margaret Mead, Andrew Wyeth.

It should be kept in mind that public or conventional schooling may not have been an option for some of these famous people, because of historical times and settings. However, for others, home education was possibly their parents' first choice, regardless of time and place. Proponents of home education assert that modern homeschooling is very similar to practices of the past. Today, many students take community field trips, read in a wide variety of challenging subject areas, experiment with apprenticeships, and interact daily with their tutoring parent(s).

The history of home education, although intriguing because of its famous key players, does not inform librarians about the current status of homeschooling, what motivates people to choose homeschooling, or types and styles of home educators. *In order to understand the "big home-schooling picture" and prepare for actively working alongside homeschoolers in our libraries, we need to look at the regional, statewide and national numbers; plus "paint some portraits" of homeschooling families.*

The startling statistics

Whenever I speak to homeschooling or library groups I begin my talk with a quick multiple choice questionnaire. My intentions are to reach out to and survey my audience, and teach in a lighthearted way. The first three questions usually refer to the estimated number of homeschoolers in a given state, and current national projections.

Audience members often breeze through the ten questions, appearing quite at ease, even smug, regarding their choices. Then I ask for the correct (or closest) answers. Their responses often *underestimate* the numbers of home educators, sometimes by thousands or hundreds of thousands!

The truth is, *homeschooling is a movement, not just an educational option.* In the late 1970s it was estimated that between ten and fifteen thousand school-aged children were taught at home in the United States.[1] Various researchers now estimate the number to be somewhere between 350,000 and 650,000. (Some spokespersons of the homeschooling movement are certain one million is a more accurate figure.) Whatever the true estimate, this represents an enormous increase in a relatively brief time. An additional fact to keep in mind: there are roughly 49 million K-12 children in public schools.

Researchers freely admit that these home-schooler tallies are estimates. There are many reasons why national and state home-schooling figures are not absolute. Some of the numbers may be skewed because:

- for some parents, homeschooling is a short lived experiment,

- homeschooling laws are different in all 50 states—some states, like Illinois, do not require homeschooling families to register or report their activities,

- nonconformist home educators do not choose to fill out state compliance forms,

- children under eight are sometimes not tallied in homeschool surveys,

- they use a broad definition of home-schooled children,

- they are based on homeschool association membership, which is voluntary.

A sampling of data from state departments of education echoes the national numbers. Student enrollment in home-based instruction has increased 920% in the past decade in Wisconsin; from 1,126 in the 1984-1985 school year, to an estimated 11,444 in 1993-1994. In Louisiana, the State Department of Education figures have gone from 796 homeschoolers registered in 1984-1985, to 3,948 in 1993-1994, nearly a 400% increase. Minnesota reported 2,322 homeschoolers in the 1987-1988 school year (the first year the state was authorized by its legislature to keep records). This total rose to 6,149 in 1992-1993, a jump of 3,827 in five years. In the southeast, North Carolina homeschoolers totalled 809 in the 1985-1986 school year, and climbed to 6,947 by 1992-1993, more than a 750% increase in eight years. The state of Washington Department of Education reports a total of 13,584 registered home educators as of January 1994, 9,539 higher than 1987. When averaged out over the last seven years, Washington homeschoolers increased at a rate of 1,362 annually. (For your information—all of these numbers are taken from state department of education statistics.)

These startling statistics illustrate a nationwide trend. Many researchers and futurists expect this pattern to continue, including John Naisbitt, who predicted the 1980s home education explosion in his book, *Megatrends: Ten New Directions Transforming Our Lives.*[2] In this classic study, Naisbitt stated, "In the 1960s and 1970s the self-help approach to education took the form of creating alternative schools; in the 1980s it will be home education."

The rapid growth of homeschooling raises several questions, including: 1) What is the significance of this trend for librarians? 2) Have librarians been forewarned of homeschooler use of libraries and home-schooling issues? In 1989, Jane Avner, writing in *School Library Journal* stated, "Today, public libraries all over the United States are noting the presence of home schoolers in their communities."[3] In 1991, a year when three excellent homeschool related articles appeared in our library literature, Theresa Gemmer was stating that "homeschooling was here to stay," and "with growth in the number of school age children, and the demonstrable success of homeschooling, we should expect an increase in families choosing this educational option in the future." Therefore, she said, "it is time that libraries and librarians take a more active role in supporting the educational efforts of homeschool families."[4]

Additionally, *The Librarian's Home Education Resource Guide* was produced by the Parent Education Services Committee of the Public Library Association in March 1991, in response to a growing interest in homeschoolers using public libraries. (This committee also published a 1993 spiral bound book entitled *Homeschoolers and the Public Library: A Resource Guide for Libraries Serving Homeschoolers.*) In an effort to hear directly from a homeschooling authority, the Adult Lifelong Learning Section of this committee sponsored a presentation by Patrick Farenga, publisher of *Growing Without Schooling*, at the 1993 American Library Association (ALA) Annual Conference in New Orleans. The title of Farenga's talk was, "Libraries & Homeschoolers: A Practical Partnership." Also, a panel discussion on homeschooling and libraries took place at the March 1994 Public Library Association meeting in Atlanta.

These professional activities and publications indicate that librarians are becoming aware of the home education movement and its potential impact on libraries. What's the next logical step? I say, without reservation, get involved or stay involved! Consequently, if we elect to take a more active role, we need to understand what motivates homeschoolers. What kind of people choose homeschooling? Why do they do so? (To benefit themselves, their children, their families, because of religious convictions, alternative lifestyles and beliefs, special needs?) What are some common teaching methods? How are religious homeschoolers different than unschoolers? What are the "politics of homeschooling?" What are some unique philosophies of home education?

A portrait of homeschoolers

Whenever I speak at library conferences, I give the audience members thirty new "serving homeschoolers ideas" in ninety minutes—a fresh notion every three minutes, with emphasis on four or five major topics. Customarily, I discuss research and trends, the wide variety of homeschooling educational styles, and who and why people choose home education.

Based on my observations, a stereotypical homeschooler or homeschooling family truly does not exist. Because no two families are alike, it is difficult to address the topic of "who" homeschools. The variations are innumerable. Nevertheless, based on my experience, I conclude mothers do the majority of tutoring, at least in the library setting. For the most part, their homeschooled children are between four- and twelve-years old, with comparatively few teenagers opting for homeschooling. (I have talked with numerous parents who tell me their young adults, usually when they are between twelve- and fourteen-years of age, approach them about re-entering or trying out public or private schools.) For further information on who chooses homeschooling, I recommend the work of two researchers listed in the endnotes to this chapter and/or the appendix—J. Gary Knowles and Brian D. Ray. Additionally, you may want to ask yourself and co-workers the question, "who homeschools in *our* community."

What motivates parents to opt for homeschooling? The reasons are limitless, so I have chosen a primary one and a spate of others. (The intention here, and in this entire book, is to raise your level of awareness about home education and homeschoolers, not to categorize or label anything or anyone.)

Although there is much discussion among researchers about the demography of homeschooling, one consistent theme stands out. The majority of people who choose the home education option do so for religious reasons. According to an article in the *Wilson Library Bulletin* by James and Suzanne LaRue, "it is estimated that 86 percent of the parents now home schooling do so for religious reasons."[5] These parents feel their Christian values are not sufficiently emphasized in public schools. In fact, many believe that American textbooks are specifically designed to undermine 'traditional values' through the promotion of secular humanism.

These Christian homeschoolers tend to have strong convictions. One such belief is that God has given them the responsibility and authority to raise and educate their children. This belief that God is intimately involved in their home schools also provides the encouragement and guidance for managing their work with children, says one researcher.[6] According to author Christopher Klicka, "In essence, the modern home school movement is a spiritual revival which has embraced the Puritan and colonial understanding of the centrality of the family in education."[7]

Other specific reasons why parents choose home education (statements in quotes are from homeschooling parents I posed questions to—the other conclusions are based on my reading and research):

- "I want to spend more time with my children,"
- low student to teacher ratio,
- to have a "warm, loving" home environment for a special needs child,
- more time for development of special talents and interests,
- to foster independent thinking children,
- family closeness and unity,
- tutorial method's superiority/accomplish more academically,
- "so I can discipline my children as I choose,"
- safety issues, overcrowding and drugs in public schools,

- so we can have "an unstructured curriculum,"
- "because we see education as inseparable from life,"
- do not agree with the bureaucratization of the schools and society,
- had problems adjusting to the public schools,
- "to teach my kids that learning is a process or journey, not just a product,"
- do not agree with the "outcome based education" teaching philosophy,
- "all ages interact together, more like the real world,"
- to avoid negative peer pressure,
- "homeschooling is helping my child develop a better self concept,"
- "because of my school and learning experiences in childhood,"
- to help a child achieve academic excellence.

In recent months, another aspect of this issue has appeared in popular periodical articles. Specifically, parents of gifted children are beginning to take their children out of the public schools. *Newsweek* magazine stated it this way; "Although there are no statistics on how many gifted students are turning to homeschooling, educators who work with such kids say they believe the number is increasing. Financially beleaguered public schools across the country have cut gifted programs in recent years, figuring that bright kids will do fine in a regular classroom. But they don't."[8]

Homeschooling educational styles

There are probably as many homeschooling educational styles as there are reasons for choosing homeschooling. Nevertheless, two are dominant. I call them the structured and unstructured styles. In some homeschooling circles these may be called the traditional and untraditional methods. For librarians, especially those who order educational materials, I feel it is important to be aware of these two primary, and some secondary, approaches to home teaching.

Homeschoolers who use a traditional approach often imitate the methods of public classroom teachers, creating lesson plans, utilizing separate textbooks for each subject, and purchasing or creating their own curriculum materials. Their school day is usually constant, starting in the morning at a specific time. A large percentage of these homeschoolers follow biblical principles and curriculum. Parents who choose the structured style of homeschooling frequently use approved correspondence courses, available from sources like A Beka (a traditional school affiliated with Pensacola Christian College), the Calvert School (has offered standard school curriculum since 1906), and Bob Jones University. This brings to mind other questions—is it our responsibility to purchase curriculum materials for our public, academic, or school library collections, so that home educators can have free and easy access to them?

On the other hand, untraditional home educators, believing that self-reliant child-centered learning works best, are far more likely to allow their children to pick their own pace of learning, or follow whatever topic fuels their curiosity and creativity. They are often skeptical of grading and standardized testing. A flexible curriculum is a comfortable fit for them; their motto might be, "the best lessons are the ones you don't prepare for." The parents (and children) tend to be open-minded, humanistic, independent thinking. They have a tendency to embrace alternative points of view and lifestyles; their choice of library books often reinforces these leanings, ranging from the importance of guardian angels to the politics of breastfeeding. Many of these untraditional homeschoolers (also called unschoolers) follow the precepts of the late John Holt. Unschoolers encourage their children to be self-directed, believing that learning thrives in an unstructured environment. Education to them is a lifelong process, only tangentially related to schools.

No matter which educational style a homeschooling family uses—structured, unstructured, traditional, untraditional, or a mix of many methods—they have one thing in common. They frequently supplement their home learning with "community school" field trips. *Community schooling*, which can be an individual, family or communal affair, happens when homeschoolers visit and actively learn in local libraries, museums, parks, playgrounds, churches and synagogues, retail and corporate businesses, 4H clubs, arboretums, science centers, and colleges and universities. (In chapter two we'll pursue this point.) These various educational excursions can be spur of the moment or pre-planned. They can also be frequent and lengthy. Homeschool parents believe these shared experiences are an integral part of their children's education and excellent exercises in socialization. To the children involved, community schooling is a fun learning experience, not an educational method.

California homeschooling parent Paige Smith, quoted in the *Live and Learn: Humboldt Homeschooler's Newsletter*, mentions three other basic educational styles:

- the "Sequenced Workbooks" approach,
- the "Unit Studies" approach,
- the "Custom Combinations" approach.

The *Sequenced Workbooks* style is characterized by the student working more "independently than in the traditional method and the teacher being available to offer assistance. The workbooks or worktexts contain information, worksheets, tests and suggestions for activities. In the *Unit Study* approach, all subjects are studied as they relate to a theme or topic. Students work in groups, co-ops, and/or independently. Unit

Studies work very well for multi-grade level teaching." When homeschoolers use a variety of educational methods, tailor made to suit their children, they are using the *Custom Combinations* option. They may lead a structured homeschool lesson on Monday, visit a nature park on Tuesday, spend five hours in the public library on Wednesday, and so on.

Minnesota homeschooler Joan Torkildson, writer and mother of two, echoes those sentiments, saying, "As far as home-schooling is concerned, I suspect most of us would fall somewhere in the middle of the continuum that places school-at-home at one end and unschooling at the other. Trouble is, there's no common name for us yet. Some describe themselves as 'eclectics'—a term I prefer because it incorporates a variety of approaches depending on mood, learning styles, time of year. Others say that they are 'muddle-of-the-roaders,' an equally appropriate description."[10] Home educators have also been categorized as "Grassroots/Child-Centered," or "Guided Child-Centered" types. (I propose a new name—the home-schoolers who integrate various approaches could be called "Independents," or "Inde-pendent Homeschoolers.")

Knowing about the different educational styles most commonly used should give you a hint of what types of library materials home educators may be searching for. Here again, because the homeschooling popu-lation is by nature diverse, their taste in library materials is quite varied. (Home educators say specifically what they would like to find in their local libraries in chapter two.) Identifying and profiling the home-schoolers in your community and region is another good way to pinpoint needs and focus collection development; more on that concept, and numerous upbeat outreach ideas in the next chapter.

The politics of home education

One of my main motivations in writing this handbook is to learn, by reading and research, how homeschooling parents and children relate to librarians, and in turn, how librarians interact with homeschoolers. On my way down that path I uncovered something interesting.

There is, indisputably, an underlying tension lurking around the homeschool movement, that more than occasionally manifests itself in the form of name calling, battle cries, capitol rallies and even court cases. The anxiety exists over a single, stalwart issue—how much regulation should a given state (or any governmental entity) place on home education? All fifty states have different laws regarding home-schooling. They each have their own name for it. North Carolina calls it non-public education, Virginia refers to it as home instruction, Louisiana labels it home study, Massachusetts calls it home education, California refers to it as home schooling, and the State of Washington labels it home-based instruction.

There are numerous burning home education political issues besides state regulation, and many distinct coalitions and viewpoints. When skirmishes occur, they usually happen at the local or state level, but not always, as witnessed by the 1994 battle over the Elementary and Secondary Education Act (ESEA), a $12 billion dollar bill designed to continue funding for programs in public and some private schools. The U. S. House of Representa-tives version (H. R. 6), and specifically the Miller amendment, were interpreted by many politically-active home educators as legislation that would potentially increase teacher certification requirements for home and other private school teachers. This was a way for the federal government to gain closer control of private schools, according to some home educators.

A coalition of homeschoolers and home-school leaders reacted to these proposed legislative changes, sending urgent faxes, calls and letters by the thousands to key congressional figures, asking them to amend H. R. 6, so that home and other private schools could ensure their freedoms and autonomy. This grass-roots effort, viewed by many homeschoolers as over-reactive, spawned a lively debate within the national homeschooling community. All things considered, the speedy and over-whelming response to H. R. 6 sent a clear reminder to national legislators that home-schoolers zealously defend their freedom of speech and freedom to teach.

The politics of home education is not a central theme of this book, but is certainly of peripheral importance. Where to locate current information on this subject and related topics, however, is very important, especially to reference librarians. For that reason, I have included a number of relevant titles and articles in the appendices of this book.

Summary

In the last two decades, mostly for religious and ideological reasons, hundreds of thousands of American families have chosen the homeschooling option. Their motivations, philosophies and educational styles are individualized yet diverse. Since *home educators will continue to use libraries extensively*, I feel it is time to prepare for and respond to the homeschoolers in our communities. Taking action now will prepare us for the future. Consequently, we need to pinpoint their needs, reach out with innovative and affordable programs and other services, and encourage them to volunteer time and energy at our libraries. A Wisconsin children's librarian says it best; "We are seeing more and more home-schoolers in our area and we need to help them as much as possible."

Endnotes

1. Lines, Patricia M. *Estimating the home schooled population* (working paper OR 91-537). Washington, D.C.: Office of Educational Research and Improvement, U.S. Department of Education. October, 1991.

2. Naisbitt, John. *Megatrends: 10 New Directions Transforming Our Lives*. New York: Warner Books Inc., 1982. p. 144.

3. Avner, Jane A. "Home Schoolers: A Forgotten Clientele." *School Library Journal*, (July 1989): 29-33.

4. Gemmer, Theresa. "The Library Response to Homeschooling." *ALIKI*, (March 1991): 20-23.

5. LaRue, James and Suzanne. "Is Anybody Home?: Home Schooling and the Library." *Wilson Library Bulletin*, (September 1991): 33-37.

6. Ray, Brian D. *A Nationwide Study of Home Education: Family Characteristics, Legal Matters, and Student Achievement*. Salem, Oregon: National Home Education Research Institute, 1990.

7. Klicka, Christopher. *The Right Choice*. Gresham, Oregon: Noble Publishing Associates, 1992. p. 123.

8. Kantrowitz, Barbara and Debra Rosenberg. "In a Class of Their Own." *Newsweek*, (January 10, 1994): 58.

9. Smith, Paige. "Home Schooling Family Styles." *Live and Learn: Humboldt Homeschooler's Newsletter*, (1994): 8-9.

10. Torkildson, Joan. "How Is Homeschooling Like a Duck-shaped Potato?" *The Grapevine: Newsletter of the Minnesota Homeschoolers Alliance*, (May/June 1994): 1.

2

Reaching Out to the Community of Homeschoolers
Determining Needs, Policies and Programs

Do you sometimes wonder what that family with three school-age children is doing in the library, or on the bookmobile, on a "school day?" Are you convinced the number of homeschoolers who use your particular library is steadily growing and that your library plays a pivotal role in the educational plans of at least a small number of homeschoolers? Do you have any idea what percentage of children within your public school district are being schooled at home? Are you ready to know more about how to link up with home educators and their children? If you're curious about the answers to these questions, willing to stretch your learning curve, ready for a new challenge and a little extra work, then it's time to tap into the homeschooling network.

Tapping into your homeschool community is no small task, as some of you may already realize. The first step is to identify the active homeschoolers in your city, county or region. But if homeschoolers come from diverse backgrounds, use a garden variety of educational styles, don't wear big H's with a picture of a house on their letter jackets, and generally defy most stereotypes, how do we locate them? Fortunately, there are time-tested ways to link up

with homeschoolers. In the following "making the connection" section, I have included a number of tips. These are based on my experience working closely with home educators in northern Wisconsin, and on creative suggestions from other librarians around the country. Variations on some of these ideas could also be used to link up with teachers from public and private schools, or general library users. Remember to keep fairness in mind—if you give extraordinary service to your library populace, including outreach or extension, a variety of programs, or any other special or unique services—offer the same to home educators.

This outreach could lead to lengthy give-and-take relationships with parents and children in your homeschool community. Later in this chapter I cite examples of this mutual exchange: homeschooled kids and their parents actively pitching in at their neighborhood libraries or library systems, volunteering on certain individualized projects (i.e. helping keep the alternative education/homeschooling resource files current), and working with Friends and other volunteers on special library projects.

Making the connection

To locate home educators in your community and region, try some of the following:

- *post an invitation on the library's community bulletin board* inviting them to sign up for a library orientation and/or reference and technology tour;

- *place announcements* in your local newspaper, at area churches (remember—roughly 75% of all home-schoolers make their educational choice because of religious convictions), professional offices, food cooperatives and other marketplaces, retail stores, Christian and independent bookstores, or wherever else you customarily promote the library;

- invite homeschoolers to the library with news releases on your local public access cable television station and radio stations;

- *attend some homeschooling confer-ences* and/or curriculum fairs to observe, gather information, meet local home educators;

- *set up a library booth* at a local, regional or statewide homeschooling conference; pass out library users' guides, storytime information, or any handouts regarding library policies for educators, and encourage home-schoolers to sign up for library instruc-tional tours;

- if a homeschooling support group meets in your library building, *ask if they are interested in hearing* (from you or another library staff member) *about new library materials and upcoming programs* for children, young adults or families;

- if you are inquisitive about a certain family that customarily uses your library during daytime hours, ask them discreetly whether they are home-schoolers (most homeschoolers will not view this as being intrusive), and invite them to further explore the library, with you or other staff as their experienced guide;

- ask your homeschooling group contact person for a copy of their "*phone and address tree*," so homeschoolers can be included in all library mailings and be forewarned of upcoming events (including the booksales, where home-schoolers search for the hard-to-find classic titles that are often cornerstones of home curriculum), or contact/join a state homeschooling association with a mailing list that includes regional home-school resource people.

Once you've made the connection

Linking up with home educators is a critical first step. If approached with some commitment, discretion and respect, leaving personal feelings aside, it may help establish the two-way communication necessary to move on to the next phases of interacting with homeschoolers in your library. These subsequent steps are:

1) developing a homeschool resource file and acquiring a core collection of home-schooling materials;

2) conducting library orientation tours, and

3) offering various programs and services for children and adults.

To maximize your chance of success, you should initiate these steps in an orderly fashion. For instance, gather information and organize your resource file first. Read reviews and acquire at least a few good books and periodicals next. Then, after those important steps are accomplished, plan the logistics of your orientation tours for homeschoolers, and what other services and programs you think would succeed. At this point you should decide, keeping your staffing circumstances and budget in mind, how much time and effort can be devoted to serving homeschoolers. (No matter what the level of commitment, home educators will appreciate your honest outreach effort.) The overall objective here, as proposed in chapter one, is to reach an "effective, high quality service level."

Your homeschooling resource file

Q. For easy, quick access by homeschoolers and librarians, where should your resource file be located?

A. It should be kept in an "accordion file" in your regular pamphlet file (in the adult reference area) and/or in a pamphlet file in the children's services area. If you intend to gather many of the items listed below, you will definitely need an expandable file. (Just an aside: an inquisitive homeschooler once asked me why we don't call those shelves "vertical files" anymore. I told him that we don't store verticals in them, and ours is now wider than it is tall!)

Q. What are the components of a complete homeschooling resource file?

A. The comprehensive resource file for homeschoolers might include:

- general information on homeschooling—different styles, methods, positive and negative aspects, personal experience anecdotes;

- current homeschooling bibliographies (include and highlight titles owned by your library—see appendix);

- copies of your state laws regarding compulsory education;

- samples of your state compliance forms that registered home-schoolers fill out (depending on the state's statutory requirements, these may be minimal or multi-page);

- phone numbers and addresses of the state department of education;

- local public school regulations, cases involving home education;

- curriculum guides from the local public school districts;

- phone numbers & addresses of home-school liaisons and curriculum administrators employed by public school districts;

- lists of local, regional, statewide, and national home education groups;

- local homeschooling support group leaders and/or contact people;

- home school publisher and supply house catalogs;

- samples of homeschooling newsletters, magazines and articles;

- handouts with "electronic connections"—homeschooling discussion and news groups on the Internet, local and regional electronic bulletin boards, companies that sell educational software (see appendix);

- articles on teaching theory, differing educational viewpoints;

- phone numbers and addresses of people authorized to give accredited tests in your state (many states do not require standardized tests);

- library card application procedures and sign-up forms and brochures spelling out special materials and services for educators;

- library volunteer application forms;

- questionnaire or personalized letter asking for recommendations on library programs and services, policies and procedures;

- information on high school equivalency tests and college entrance examinations.

This readily accessible, complete resource file on homeschooling serves two purposes. It gives reference and children's librarians a great starting point for information searches and a place to put current and classic home education clippings, and provides parents at all levels of homeschool experience an opportunity to peruse and compare their information with resource file material. (Another good idea: the King

County Library System in the Seattle, Washington area puts compact, individualized homeschool "information packets" in their resource file for homeschooling parents to pick up, take home, keep.) In order to gather current information for your file, you will need to: A) contact the liaisons listed on the preceding bulleted list; B) inspect homeschooling resource books like Theodore Wade's *The Home School Manual* (5th edition),[1] Mary Pride's *Big Book of Home Learning*,[2] and the *Home School Handbook* by Mark and Helen Hegener;[3] C) "pick the brain" of your favorite in-house reference librarian and/or D) consult the appendices of this book.

One further reflection—if your library is large enough for this to work, consider having one person on staff be the homeschool "expert." This person could be a children's librarian, a reference department professional, a librarian who homeschools, or another qualified staff member with an interest or curiosity in the subject. This gives home educators a specific contact person to deal with about interlibrary loan requests, collection development, test proctoring, library tours, new resources, and other important issues. It also simplifies and clarifies the two-way communication, which should always be a primary concern.

Orientation tours for homeschoolers

The intent of homeschooler orientation tours is to teach library skills, acquaint homeschoolers with your library facility and collection, and ultimately to increase user confidence. Orientated family members would eventually do their own searches and research, and take advantage of the full spectrum of library services, easing the burden on reference and children's librarians. Since you probably already conduct instructional tours (whether loosely or highly organized) for many other new library users, good procedures may already be in place. To orientate

homeschoolers you should stick with those general procedures and think about testing out or implementing some of the following ideas.

During the orientation tour your strategy should include the following:

1. Give homeschooling families a general tour of the library, featuring the new or recently updated homeschooling resource file, any books or periodical articles on homeschooling and/or educational methods;

2. Explain the online or card catalog, and give handouts that show, with diagrams, arrows, etc., how to navigate the automated system;

3. Ask them about their specific interests, and keep a record of these comments;

4. Finally, explain the fundamental policies of your library and library system, emphasize the importance and reasoning behind having a balanced collection and the role the library plays in the city and region, and share handouts that illustrate library policies/services.

Your strategy may also include these ten tips:

1. Focus on the reference materials in the children's department;

2. Profile two or three high quality periodicals for young people;

3. Summarize library programming for children and young adults;

4. Share a few books that would help the homeschooling family develop better library research skills;

5. Give a thorough reference and technology tour, showing CD-ROM stations, microfilm machines, dial-in access procedures, any online services available, education-related reference materials (in print or online), and the processes and limitations of interlibrary loan; (I also pass out a list of "Reference Books That Open The Door To Learning" at this

time, a booklist covering at least a few special subject fields appealing to homeschoolers;)

6. Pass out and explain "reference pathfinders;"

7. Show a variety of multimedia items, including compact discs, audio and videotapes, machines for special needs customers (Kurzweil, etc.) and underscore the importance of library media services;

8. Hand out "assignment alert forms" and explain the relationship between unit studies and subject area depletion;

9. Introduce key library staff who may, because of their particular responsibilities, interact regularly with home educators;

10. Tour available library meeting rooms and explain scheduling procedures.

Time-tested programs and services

When the Tulsa City-County Library (TCCL) "Service to Homeschoolers" Task Force was commissioned last year to investigate whether their local homeschoolers were being served at least as well as children attending public and other private schools, they weren't sure what the findings would be. After surveying library literature, analyzing TCCL services currently offered, and querying other libraries about their homeschooling resources and programs, task force members concluded that services for Tulsa area homeschoolers could be expanded and improved. Consequently, they recommended:

• reaching out to area homeschool groups and individuals;

• improving library catalogs and collections;

• making a special effort to increase communication and remove barriers by better educating library staff.

The Tulsa City-County Library Board and administration recently analyzed the task force results and decided to implement the numerous recommendations. Consequently, one of TCCL's prime objectives in 1995-1996 will be to link up with and provide services to area homeschoolers. For practical purposes, they will use the task force recommendations as a roadmap, making changes and improvements based on its contents.

In the next section we will examine samples of successful and innovative programs. Hopefully, these examples will help you unleash some fresh ideas of your own. To obtain this information, and the homeschooler's comments later in this chapter, I sent out scores of surveys to people in all corners of the country, and a handful to Canada. I also posted questions to three lively library discussion groups on the Internet and researched a number of periodical articles and books.

Programming examples and ideas

It is important to alert your area homeschoolers and regional homeschool associations whenever you're kicking off a regular storytime season, the popular summer library program, book discussion groups, or any other programs geared for a general library audience. Additionally, if you or your staff have the time and money to offer unique programming for homeschoolers, here are some ideas intended to get your creative juices flowing. You may want to experiment with a variation on one of these themes or design your own special program. To be successful, exploit the individual talents of your library programmers and listen to the wishes of the potential homeschooling audience. After that, think once again about your available human resources and:

• initiate a young adult book discussion group, using the Junior Great Books series as a framework;

• sponsor a multi-session workshop for a homeschool association or a general audience of home educators—include workshops on how to get the most out of your automated system using tips, shortcuts and search strategies, how to master CD-ROM products, print reference sources, and feature an electronic "treasure hunt;"

- conduct workshop programs on how to sharpen library research skills designed for homeschooling parents and their children;

- schedule school-age storytimes or "librarytimes" at nontraditional times to attract homeschool kids and young adults;

- experiment with intergenerational programs of all types;

- sponsor a speaker who is a well-known homeschooling authority;

- sponsor a child development specialist from your local college or university to speak on his/her expertise, or invite other community people to share their skills;

- coordinate the publicity for a home-school theater performance happening at your library;

- co-sponsor a children's puppet theater show that premieres in your library auditorium or meeting room;

- host a panel discussion with representatives from public, private, home, parochial, charter and alternative schools.

Additional potential homeschooling program topics mentioned in survey responses were: folktales, anything musical or artistic, local author talks and book discussions, how to take notes, basic reference orientations for children, creative writing, math and science, booktalks, library policies and intellectual freedom. For more original ideas, ask your homeschoolers!

Hopefully you are beginning to see some common threads winding throughout and binding all these new outreach ideas together. For me, a quote from a Massachu-setts librarian aptly sums it up. Thinking back to times when she worked with homeschoolers, she noted that, "often a homeschooling parent would be very tentative at first and she (as it usually turned out) was pleasantly surprised to find that I did not sit in judgment of her educational choice. It was important for them to feel welcomed (as it is with all patrons); I don't think they would volunteer or join book discussion groups, story hours, etc., without real outreach to them."

Service examples and ideas

What types of services besides programs are being offered to homeschoolers across the country? Is there a whirl of activity, or is most of the action happening in a small percentage of libraries? Are these libraries expanding services because their homeschooling population is booming? What about the cost of serving homeschoolers? Should our library finances in the 1990s, a time of austere cutbacks and budgetary constraints, be spent on outreach to groups like homeschoolers? If there may be extra expenses because of new services offered, how much are we, or our library board, willing to spend to initiate or increase services for home educators? In other words, before you decide on the "effective, high quality service level" you're comfortable with, some tough questions need to be addressed.

At this time, a definitive study pinpointing the percentage of libraries or library systems analyzing and/or upgrading services to homeschoolers does not exist. In the scheme of things, keeping in mind the importance of "doing versus knowing," would such a study be valuable? Should you base a decision on it? I say no to both questions. Perhaps your decision should be based on the number of homeschoolers using your library (in other words—service demand). Or maybe it should be tied to your particular financial capabilities, and long-range plans relating to programming? Additionally, it is not clear how much is already being done for this steadily growing user group, or if libraries with brisk homeschooling patronage are placing more emphasis on special programs and services than libraries with minimal home educator interaction. In my opinion, when it's time to expand services to home educators, you will feel compelled to take action.

Regardless of these unanswered (or unanswerable) questions, one thing is clear. *Imaginative, inexpensive, cooperative, and trend setting services already exist in many libraries throughout the country.* In preparing this book, I initiated a survey (see appendix IX) of selected libraries in ten states and Canada to collect examples of the types of programs currently offered to homeschoolers. There is great value in these individual ideas, and even greater value when viewed as a whole. These time tested (but not foolproof), practical examples, from librarians who have experience working with homeschoolers, can be catalysts to change in your library. So once again, for firsthand information about homeschool programs and services, we go directly to the source, to the words of library colleagues.

❧ When I worked in the Reading (PA) Public Library we had a bunch of homeschoolers use the library. I helped one woman who had a boy with profound learning disabilities. Because he had a hard time with reading and reading comprehension, the mother and I worked out a film series for him using the resources of the Pennsylvania Public Library Film Center. She chose the films and I'd work on scheduling them with the Film Center. I think this is a good example that shows how a library can really work with a homeschooling parent to get what they and their child really need, stuff they wouldn't be able to get on their own, or at least for free.❧

❧ We are declaring April as 'Homeschoolers Month' at the Arlington Heights (IL) Public Library and will be offering specialized tours to all home-schoolers during the month. I hope we get a big response!❧

❧ We are swamped by homeschoolers and by grandparent and parent tutors and, of course, by every other variety of library patron. We have arranged a display of 'books' the homeschooled children had written and illustrated. We also circulated a homemade book for a brief period (it wouldn't hold up to much circulation). The creators were thrilled to see their book checked out.❧ (TN)

❧ I like the idea of targeting homeschooling populations and intentionally supplementing their curricula with materials that can also be used by the public-at-large (focused collection development).❧ (IL)

❧ We have just received a grant from the state (TN) in a new category called 'intergenerational learning.' With the money, I intend to establish a Family Learning Center. This will consist of a specific area in the library with tables, chairs, bookshelves and learning materials. Of course, any patron may use such a facility, but it is aimed at two specific groups: homeschoolers *and* those parents attempting to work with public school children who are having some difficulty in school. We expect to provide materials for the children and teaching aids for adults on several levels. (Some parents are nearly illiterate and they want desperately to be able to help their children.) We expect cooperation from several local groups and we hope to eventually include some volunteers as tutors.❧

❧ In Burlington (VT), librarians ordered subscriptions of teaching magazines and educational books and other materials were also made available. Community rooms were used as homeschool classrooms and special programs were run during the day, as well as after school.❧

❧ In our branch library in Flint (MI), I have had two interactions with parents who are homeschoolers. The positive experience was working with a person with a low income who was extremely happy that a library moved into her neighborhood. Library materials save her a lot in book and other material costs. I have passed on discarded periodicals that she uses in her teaching. She has also requested materials from other libraries through our inter-delivery service. She is a taxpayer in the county and this enables her to use library services."

" Thus far, the only things I have done for homeschoolers are attend one of their meetings to advertise the library, and pass out a booklist especially designed for homeschoolers, with manuals and tip books. I have also ordered as many books on the subject as I ' could find. I think also that by just making the effort to say 'we are here and understand that books are difficult to find' is helpful." (PA)

" Our collection is developing due to questions and concerns posted by homeschoolers. Homeschooling parents are very enthusiastic about the prospect of helpful materials being acquired by the library. We will continue to offer competent, courteous, thorough service to the homeschoolers in the community, and will acquire resources for them. We are planning to expand services to this group and will continue to listen to other suggestions. One suggestion to our Internet Coordinator involves giving patrons access to a homeschooling news group." (PA)

" We do not try to seek out homeschoolers, but we reach out to serve them if we can. Most are very grateful for library services. We recently made a list of materials in our library of special interest to homeschoolers. We offer teacher's cards to homeschooling parents which give them extended loan periods and increase the limit of books allowed for checkout. Generally, we offer homeschool teachers the same benefits as public school teachers." (IL)

" Homeschoolers come to our small library for light and entertaining reading. Most are very friendly and supportive of the library and they spread the word about the bookmobile." (MN)

" We do have curriculum guides from the public schools on file here. We only have elementary age homeschoolers; by high school they pretty much are in the schools." (IL)

" The homeschoolers are thrilled to have computer access for their students at the library. They also like to be included in the Summer Reading Program— they can do it all at home (book logs, prizes, etc.) if they don't want to attend the scheduled events at the library." (MN)

" We are in the process of developing a policy for extended loan to homeschoolers." (IL)

" We don't consciously buy curricular support materials, but do buy materials which can support juvenile learning. Our ILL service is very helpful for them." (MN)

" While I don't embrace the philosophy of homeschooling, I can see where it has merits, and feel my obligation to provide materials to meet the needs of all segments of our tax paying society! I have no objection to providing materials that would interest them and have purchased many of the study guides, such as the Mary Pride series.

We also purchase a large number of novels for both children and adults from a Christian bookseller; they are in heavy demand by the homeschooling families but are equally enjoyed by as many other readers. I'm very aware of their needs and consciously purchase nonfiction materials I think they would need. I feel more of an obligation to have an up-to-date nonfiction section for their needs." (MN)

" I'm not ready to buy homeschooling curricula, but we do purchase our materials with homeschoolers in mind. We try to collect material that has wide

A Guide to Homeschooling for Librarians

appeal or usefulness. We did order a set of geography videos at the request of homeschooling families." (IL)

" Our library carries the periodical *Growing Without Schooling*, serves as a meeting place for the regional homeschooling support group, and provides the space for a number of other homeschool family activities, including Suzuki violin concerts, science and art shows, and the annual homeschooler puppet show. We also purchase classic and some current homeschooling books, and encourage collection development suggestions from homeschool kids and parents. To keep in touch, we periodically send out a quick note to the homeschool association or contact person, mentioning upcoming events and programs." (WI)

" At the Renton (WA) Public Library the librarian arranges tours of the branch in cooperation with the children's librarian. She leads the adult tour while the children are able to explore items of interest to them with the children's librarian. "I find homeschoolers great to work with and highly motivated people. They really rely on and appreciate us."

" Our teacher loan policy currently does not include homeschooling teachers as 'teachers,' and therefore doesn't allow for extended loan check-out. We are currently revising our policy. I would like to see our teacher loan policy revised to include homeschooling teachers, and extend the check-out time from four to six weeks." (IL)

" At our small public library, we maintain a pamphlet file of newspaper clippings, homeschooling laws, and miscellaneous other items relating to the subject. Homeschool kids have also exhibited samples of their work in our window display. We keep an updated list of home educators in our two-county region, and occasionally put together brief homeschooling bibliographies. A few years ago we handed out a needs assessment survey to them; they provided us with some very good

suggestions, compliments and criticisms." (WI)

" The homeschoolers in this area have made very little use of the public library. Of course if they made a special request for a program or materials, I would do the best I could to provide it, as I do for all the general public." (MN)

" They are great participators in our existing programs—clubs, contests, workshops, presentations. They volunteer—both adults and children. They use us as a forum. I feel homeschoolers have done as much for the library as we have done for them. They provide us with homeschooling information for the public, present workshops on various homeschooling topics, and use the library as a showcase for displays. They also present programs during National Library Week and on other special occasions (some are on the arts, others on educational issues)." (PA)

" They appreciated our video collection, which emphasized documentaries and classics. We should invite homeschoolers to join our Friends groups—they have a lot to contribute!" (MN)

The preceding real life examples of services and activities are merely a sampling of what is happening in libraries. Here are still more intriguing ideas:

- put together an author club for kids;

- hold seasonal daytime open houses at library branches;

- show daytime educational films for youngsters over seven years old;

- create flyers to advertise special services;

- compose and distribute a "guidelines to use when choosing books for children" brochure;

- start a parent/teacher special collection;

- co-present an educational program at the library, with a homeschooling parent;

- conduct an in-service program on home-schooling, designed for staff in your library, branches and/or library system.

Homeschoolers speak out about library services

One of the surefire ways to determine what services any of our library customers regard as vital is to ask them. Pat Farenga is the publisher of *Growing Without Schooling* (*GWS*) and President of Holt Associates. He realized that librarians and home-schoolers were becoming more aware of each other, and he included a "Survey about Library Use" in a 1992 *GWS* issue. This questionnaire was also initiated so responses could be passed on to library professionals attending the annual American Library Association Conference, where Farenga would be speaking. Generally, the survey encouraged home-schoolers to share ideas about how libraries could better serve them, *and* how home-schoolers could help libraries. Specific main topics included: homeschool vertical file packets, library tours, instructional workshops, curriculum guides, displays and exhibits, volunteering, materials, positive and negative aspects about libraries. A number of months later, the original questions, and responses from homeschooling parents, were published in *GWS*. These results should, along with the aforementioned two dozen firsthand examples, help you decide what services to emphasize in your library. The *Growing Without Schooling* "Survey about Library Use" concluded that:

- less than 30% of the respondents had access to a homeschool resource file in their library, but 59% would like to have it;

- 50% of the homeschoolers did not take advantage of available library instructional tours;

- 34% would like to be able to take library "workshops" on databases, encyclopedias, reference books;

- 2% of the respondents used curriculum guides at their library, but 73% would like the opportunity to do so;

- "displays of homeschooler projects" occurred in 39% of the libraries;

- 30% of the respondents volunteer at their library, while 52% could but don't, and 18% would like volunteer opportunities made available;

- children's fiction and nonfiction, including classics and easy readers, are heavily used by homeschoolers;

- books on games, toys, science projects, and the practice of homeschooling are important;

- video and audio tapes, biographies and general history books are also commonly used.

The ten most requested topics for books and materials were:

1. homeschooling books in general,
2. math and science,
3. Christian homeschooling,
4. educational videos,
5. Raymond Moore books,
6. John Holt books,
7. curriculum guides,
8. *Home Education* magazine,
9. *Growing Without Schooling* magazine,
10. Mary Pride books.

What homeschoolers "liked best about their libraries" was:

1. friendly, helpful staff who take an interest in homeschooling;
2. interlibrary loans;
3. good selection of children's books and materials;
4. friendly environment;
5. well-organized children's programs;
6. use of rooms for homeschooling meetings;
7. one month or longer loan period;

8. no limit to number of books you can check out;

9. periodicals to check out.

What homeschoolers "liked least about their libraries" was:

1. unfriendly, intrusive, or difficult librarians;

2. budget cuts;

3. not enough space;

4. lack of materials;

5. disposing of card catalogs in favor of computer systems;

6. throwing away or burning books;

7. services not well publicized;

8. not enough Christian materials;

9. limited hours;

10. catalogs don't cross-reference "home-schooling" as a topic.

During the information gathering process of this book project I sent out a questionnaire entitled *Improving My Public Library: A Survey for Homeschoolers.* As with Pat Farenga's survey, my intent was to encourage people who teach their children at home to speak out candidly on the issue of library service to homeschoolers. As it turned out, they were pleasantly surprised to be asked for their input and quite willing to offer suggestions. Once again, these comments may help you formulate a home-schooling service plan, plus generate more practical and inexpensive ideas for serving the general public. Here are suggestions for us, from the pens of homeschoolers:

❝ Maybe librarians could 'keep an ear to the ground' regarding local events (i.e., theater productions, children's work-shops, etc.) and order appropriate books in anticipation.❞

❝ I would like to be able to make requests for new book purchases—especially more biographies, historical fiction, classics. There are some beautifully illustrated science books that I would like to borrow.❞

❝ I feel like there is more available to me than I am aware of—would like to know how I can best use my library. I would love for my librarian to give maybe a one-time class on what is available. It would be fun for me to have my librarian take a sample topic, as for a unit study, and show how we can develop it using a variety of reference materials and tools.❞

❝ More programming for day time—don't make it exclusively for homeschool-ers—include everyone.❞

❝ More multicultural fiction/nonfiction for children & adults.❞

❝ Another nice feature would be 'travel or sick kits,' where the librarian puts together materials for an individual.❞

❝ Perhaps sponsor activities such as 'sci-ence by mail' at the library—home-schoolers and others could be involved.❞

❝ For 2-1/2 years I homeschooled our daughter and used the library as a sec-ond classroom. We found everything we needed, in addition to having the children's and reference librarians take a personal interest in our progress. Subscriptions to teaching magazines were made available, community rooms could be used as classrooms, special programs were run during the day, as well as 'after school' hours.❞

❝ Libraries need to offer more programs for children who are seven to fifteen years old.❞

❝ A couple years ago I asked our librar-ian about setting up a library display on homeschooling. She welcomed the idea, so I reserved some time for the display case and gathered up various homeschooling books and publica-tions, and some projects, photos, and artwork that reflected our learning and interests. We also included a few quotes from John Holt and a listing of famous people who were educated at home. The children, utilizing their unique artistic talents, designed a poster that read "Homeschooling—A

Good Choice." People are often confused and curious about educating children outside the traditional school setting. A simple library display can be an excellent way to educate them about homeschooling.❞

❝ I'd like to be made aware of the services available to public school teachers, and have the same privileges. It would be real nice to be able to reserve more than three books—three is not very many when it comes to planning unit studies.❞

❝ The books in our library could be so much better. I guess you have to have the Babysitter Club books and biographies of Madonna and Janet Jackson, but what about the great, classical books? Do you know where homeschoolers find them? People have actually started cottage industries by going to book sales at public libraries, buying these great books and then reselling them at homeschooling conventions! Please keep these great books. Put the Babysitter Club books on the lower shelf in the corner (those who are hooked will find them), and bring out *Freckles, Robinson Crusoe, Little Women, Heidi*, etc. I still remember wanting to rush to the public library after attending a home education workshop on a literature-based unit study approach. 'These books will be in your public library,' the presenter kept saying. 'These are great, classical works that have stood the test of time,' she added. So, the morning after I eagerly started my search. An hour later, I was frustrated. At least three-quarters of the books on the workshop list were not in the library. Some of those available turned out to be adaptations or watered-down versions. I'm not talking about Christian books—these are just good books. Also, I take home education catalogues to the library to see what the library has—its always been very disappointing.❞

❝ Reference books like the 'Usborne books' would be great! (I remember trying to ask the librarian about those—

she looked pretty puzzled.) Our library has some of these, and other practical reference books for kids, but usually just one copy is shared by the system, and/or several libraries, and many times the books are checked out, or on reserve.❞

❝ I would like libraries to have home education books for adults such as: *For the Children's Sake*, by Susan Schaeffer Macauley; *Honey for a Child's Heart,* by Gladys Hunt; *Books Children Love*, by Elizabeth Wilson; *Teaching Children*, by Diane Lopez.❞

❝ I love the dial-in access, especially since we have an active infant. I can look up books at home and then go to the library with my list. Also, it helps to request a book before I go to the library so I don't get home and get a call that it's in. The automated services are great—no wasted time on the phone.❞

❝ Reference librarians have always been helpful. However, I'm not sure what is proper to ask. They are always accommodating but is it really alright to ask for the top ten most popular baby names?! I'm sure they're rolling their eyes.❞

❝ It's probably no surprise, but the way to improve the library is to get good librarians who are willing to listen to your needs. We *love* one of the librarians at our main library. She sets aside books for my kids and calls me when she sees something I might like. We send her Christmas cards, birth announcements—anything to stay friendly with her! She has been a great help to my kids' education. Our home education is based on good, classic literature, so I can't tell you what it means to have a resource like Theresa!❞

❝ If the people in charge of ordering books could attend just one home school workshop, I think they'd have a better idea of home education, and our needs. The books we are interested in, and our basic philosophies of education, would be so clear. We really aren't a bunch of overprotective parents who

A Guide to Homeschooling for Librarians

want to ban *Ramona Quimby* from the library; we really just want to provide our kids with the best, well-rounded education available. Almost 100 percent of the time, that education includes frequent use of the public library."

" I think home educators would be interested in year-round reading programs or even book clubs/discussions (like storytimes for older children). Homeschoolers could come to the library during the day, which may be downtime in the children's area. Kids could meet together and present book reports to each other (e.g., "Reading Rainbow"), or the librarians could whet kids' reading appetites with various recommendations. You wouldn't have to have all the 'bells and whistles' of a summer reading program; just have a regular meeting time and place. Home school families could even take turns hosting it, and/or putting on puppet shows for each other, etc."

" A training session for home educators would be helpful. Maybe have a few hours some late summer/early fall where home school parents could be invited to the library to learn the 'ins and outs.' Public school teachers learn about their school libraries—the public library is the home educator's library. Librarians could give a general overview of the library and then tell us about lesser-known aids and references. For example, our library has a three-ring notebook in which the librarians categorize the books (i.e., if you love *Little House* books, you'll like *Sarah, Plain and Tall*). This is a great resource, but it took me two years to hear about it. I also didn't realize that the easy readers and picture books were labeled on the spine with different-colored tape to indicate they are Christmas, Thanksgiving books, etc. I don't think this stuff is something librarians want to keep secret, it's just that consumers don't even *know* about it."

" A play area in the library for younger kids is a great help for large families

(which seems to be the case for many homeschool families)."

" Voice activated renewal, dial-in access, and the printed lists of date dues are all things our library has added, and we love them."

" I would appreciate it if the local library had more communication with the school library. I would like to be able to use some of the schools' instructional materials."

" Because we don't use textbooks at home, I rely on the library for historical fiction and science trade books. I wish our library could afford some of the quality kids magazines which are available. I would also like them to subscribe to some homeschooling journals. I think our librarian does very well, considering budget limitations."

" I wish we had a larger collection, that ILL books arrived faster and could be checked out longer, and that the audiotape collection was larger. We use our library system books a lot; I wish more books arrived from them, more quickly."

" Our family uses the interlibrary loan system almost weekly. Because of our small library's collection, we have to use the ILL to respond to our children's changing interests."

" I would like to have a vehicle for suggesting library purchases. Also, I feel that the numerous libraries we frequent should purchase quality children's books. They seem to add to their collection on an ongoing basis, nonfiction and fiction, in a balanced way. However, numerous times I have gotten notices on books I have returned; I am always pleased with their offer to double-check and they usually find the book. It would be nice to have more children's book discussions, for a variety of age levels."

" Our family sees the use of libraries as the cornerstone of our homeschooling. We regularly use the bookmobile, two local/regional libraries, the library system, a college library, and interlibrary loan services. Due to the fact that we buy our own home school materials, (and many of us design our own curricula), I use interlibrary loan to preview possible purchases. I get lots of catalogs of books and learning materials, and keep abreast of the children's book market. I occasionally suggest purchases to the librarian and usually see these titles on the shelf not long thereafter."

"We have used the library as a meeting place for our regional homeschoolers group. Our librarian was gracious enough to attend those meetings on several occasions to explain/share resources we might not have known about. He also listened to our suggestions and concerns. Homeschooling books and periodicals have also been purchased by the library system, in response to our needs. We especially look forward to the bookmobile as they seem to have lots of new children's books. I look around me and see lots of home-schoolers making the effort to get to the bookmobile, and checking out armfuls of books—and putting them to good use."

"We have recently acquired an IBM compatible computer and would be interested in borrowing software, if it becomes available at the library."

"We would love to use the library for homeschool classes. Many of us live south of town, and others north. It would be a centrally-located learning space for us."

"We would like IBM software, more 'Eyewitness books,' the Brown Paper School Book series, and more current titles that tell about the 'best' books for your children."

"We would like to see sample curricula and programs from varied companies, especially the phonics programs. Also, we would like magazines like *Kids Art News, Backyard Scientist, Growing Without Schooling*, plus videos like the Joseph Campbell and Bill Moyers

series, and more foreign language (especially Spanish) materials for adults and kids."

"Many of the kids write book reviews. Could there be a library place where these could be displayed, where other kids could see them and get ideas of books they might want to read? Could you use the older kids in the library as volunteers?"

"I would like more books in the library that have something to say about how kids can learn to understand themselves, their uniqueness and place in the world. Also, more books on music, mathematics, the arts, communication."

Why aren't *your* kids in school today?

Whenever I talk to groups of librarians about locating, linking up with, and serving home educators, I share this personal anecdote about how *not* to reach out to homeschoolers.

Back in the early years of my professional career, I worked at a certain public library where nosiness was a common, expected and acceptable practice, as natural as reader's advisory and the card registration process. In this particular workplace, where the small staff functioned as if they were a large family unit, it was customary to privately ask co-workers personal, even intimate questions. Needless to say, with a few exceptions, this openness allowed us to become well informed about the lives of our colleagues (and drastically reduced the need for personal counseling services).

Unfortunately, one staff member carried this philosophy of communication and candor even farther. She regularly chatted and gossiped with library customers, before, during and after the circulation checkout process. Consequently, she learned about the lifestyles of their college-age sons and daughters, family financial stability or insolvency, religious and other preferences, and so on. Many of these queries were loudly announced without thinking about the patron's feelings, privacy needs or other irreconcilable consequences. On more than one occasion, this library staff member, upon noticing school-age children in the library with their dad and/or mom on a "regular" public school day, blurted out, "why aren't *your* kids in school today!?" No matter how she uttered this phrase, no matter what word was emphasized, it didn't come out sounding good. It sounded intrusive, unreserved and forward, especially if she had not met the parties she was addressing. When asked this particular question, the alert home educator parent sometimes responded with, "we are in school today—at your library," or, "the library is our classroom." It caught most of them by surprise, and left them at a loss for words. Either way, the blunt question caused homeschoolers to be perplexed and uncomfortable. It also seemed, in my opinion, to intrude on "their private space."

Because home educators are sometimes sensitive to criticism and conjecture, exercising a bit of verbal restraint could pay big rewards.

In my experience, one reason home-schooling parents may have a difficult time dealing with and responding to sensitive questions like, "why aren't *your* kids in school today?," is they need a certain amount of mutual trust and respect to be established first. With this in mind, librarians interacting with home educators could become well-informed about, and sensitive to, homeschooling stereotypes (as with all other broad-brush opinions and stereotypes), i.e., all homeschool kids lack social skills and companionship, homespun curricula never work, all home educators teach alike, home educators are either straight-as-an-arrow conservatives or ex-hippies, home schools are less effective than public and other private schools, and homeschoolers are religious fanatics. From my point of view, and based on the survey comments and experiences of many other

librarians and homeschoolers, these are oversimplified opinions and unfair generalizations. Additionally, if anyone has a personal bias about homeschoolers or homeschooling, those feelings should be kept out of the library workplace.

Conversely, and just as importantly, home-schoolers could make a concerted effort to know the needs and philosophies of librarians, including intellectual freedom and collection development issues. Do homeschoolers know what we mean by a "balanced collection?" This would naturally foster better communication and understanding between the two groups, and diminish the possibility of a contentious relationship. When this two-way effort clicks, a positive link could be established; both parties can then begin to work together in a mutually advantageous way.

I address this linking or "bridge building" topic whenever I speak to regional home-schooling associations with a talk entitled, "Insider's Secrets On How to Best Use Your Public Library." During this sixty-minute presentation I touch on the following, with an emphasis on the first two points:

- *how to communicate/interact with library staff*;
- *volunteering at your local library*;
- taming the technological tiger that lives in your library;
- great "old and new" reference materials;
- classic and current home education materials;
- keeping a library activity log;
- intellectual freedom and censorship;
- accessing and using the library via home computer/modem;
- available educational computer software;
- library programs for the "young and older;"
- the home education resource file.

Homeschool parents present at these talks listen to my ardent wanderings and opinions, including this refrain—"the most effective way to assure yourself of great service is to actively volunteer at your local library. As an inside volunteer, you will see through new eyes. You will be more aware of library opportunities."

They also review an explanatory handout called, "A Dozen Interesting Ways You Could Help At Your Local Library," which features the following ideas:

- put together an annual puppet or magic show, and/or help with the busy summer reading program;

- read and review a book for your children's/YA librarians;

- originate and sponsor an art or science show using materials and projects created by your homeschool kids;

- help librarians originate and/or maintain a comprehensive home-schooling resource file;

- pick and clip periodical articles for the general pamphlet file;

- donate books or other materials you feel would round out the library collection;

- assist the Friends group with their fund raising efforts;

- coordinate an artistic or informational window display/exhibit at the library;

- help reshelve books and other materials, process periodicals and pamphlets, repair "hurt" books, and do keyboarding/typing;

- assist with a retrospective conversion and/or automation project;

- become a library board trustee or Friends board member;

- volunteer, with your teenagers, on the library bookmobile;

- be an outspoken advocate for the library.

Summary

This chapter has concentrated on reaching out to people in your homeschooling community through a variety of programs, services, cooperation and communication. Now it's time to peek at the flip side of the coin. In chapter three, we will examine the challenges of serving home educators.

Endnotes

1. Wade, Theodore. *The Home School Manual: Plans, Pointers, Reasons and Resources*. Niles, MI: Gazelle Publications, 1993.

2. Pride, Mary. *Big Book of Home Learning*. Wheaton, IL: Crossway Books, 1991.

3. Hegener, Mark and Helen. *Homeschool Handbook*. Tonasket, WA: Home Education Press, 1994.

3

The Challenges of Serving Homeschoolers
Critical Issues in Planning Services

This chapter will raise puzzling and practical questions, acquaint you with challenging issues librarians have experienced, and recommend sensible solutions to both. As in previous chapters, you will find many common themes interweaving throughout. Even though they originate with 40 different people, the real-life anecdotes focus on only a handful of themes. You may want to pay particular attention to these reoccurring ones. They are more likely to become issues at *your* library.

Working alongside home educators in the library is occasionally an unpredictable, challenging experience. Just like other customers, they may doggedly pursue a censorship cause, demand special treatment, provoke frontline staff, or attempt to manipulate or circumvent library policy. In my opinion, these instances are not common, but they do happen. Also, in order to work well with homeschoolers, we should keep the concept of a judicial scale (or balance) in mind. For instance: 1) how do we fairly balance the basic and unique service needs of homeschoolers with those of other library users? 2) Do we purchase specific curriculum materials for home educator parents if we already offer the same service for private and public school

teachers? 3) What about the delicate balance between censorship and collection development, exclusion versus inclusion? 4) At what crucial stage(s) in the challenge process does healthy criticism become a negative censorship issue?

Censorship issues

In the future, will debate about censorship be the major flashpoint between librarians and homeschoolers? Do homeschoolers understand, or will they ever understand, our passionate feelings about intellectual freedom and censorship? Are most challenges intended to deny access to materials and ideas, or merely objections or denunciations voiced in the spirit of giving birth to a pregnant opinion?

Working with homeschoolers in public libraries over the past seven years, I have only experienced one instance of a home-school parent filling out a "Request for Reconsideration" form. When I chatted with this particular parent, it was clear she was not interested in having the material pulled from the library collection. She simply wanted her feelings to be known. In my past and current experience, far more censorship-related skirmishes occur with library customers who are not home-schoolers. Many library professionals, however, deal with unique critiques and complaints from homeschoolers, as witnessed by examples later in this chapter. Challenges intended to deny access to materials also occur in some libraries. According to colleagues responding to my surveys, these are often, but not always, initiated by people with fundamentalist religious viewpoints.

When you reflect back, how many full-blown censorship challenges have occurred at *your* library in the past ten years? How many were protests that didn't reach the censorship level? What percentage of these incidents actually involved home educators? Thinking back again, and being thoroughly honest, how often do *we* refrain from purchasing materials homeschoolers or others may object to? Do we regularly shy away from disagreement and debate, thinking it will inevitably lead to a book being taken permanently off the shelves? When you read through the "real-life experiences" later in this chapter, look for examples of preselection censorship (also known colloquially as "dodging the hot potato"), resistance to wrestling with challenges, *and* outspoken opinions of some home educators.

We need to consistently address home-schooler censorship issues which arise. They tend to be, like challenges from other library customers, the little red buttons that buzz us awake from our complacency and keep us at the ready. They also continually remind us we need to take action and make sensible, unwavering decisions (in the case of actual censorship battles), or simply alert us that someone cares enough about an issue to make a fuss. I don't know about you, but when homeschoolers or other library customers boldly state their view-point, with no intent or desire to deny access to materials, I feel grateful for the wake-up call. In my opinion, constructive criticism from people outside the library

workplace or library board often encourages us to refine and improve outdated, fundamentally weak, and/or shortsighted library policies and procedures.

More practical questions and reflections

Furthermore, we should consider and debate these eight important questions. (I will comment more on these, following the "real-life experiences" portion of this chapter.) 1) What are a public school district's statutory responsibilities for providing instructional materials for home based educators? 2) How can public librarians work with school librarians to understand and help meet the curriculum needs of homeschoolers? 3) Is "curriculum support" the best way to go? 4) Do unsupervised homeschool children at your library really pose a big problem for staff and others? 5) Do the scales of fairness tip toward abuse when a homeschooling family wants thirteen items at a time through interlibrary loan, with absolutely no substitutions? 6) Should educators using your library, whether they are public, private or homeschool, receive special treatment? 7) Do some of us have an "attitude problem" or bias regarding home-schoolers and homeschooling, or toward public, parochial or other private school teachers and schools? 8) Furthermore, in times of tight library budgets, can we justify expanding our library collections or developing unique programs to meet the specific needs of homeschoolers or other small groups of library customers?

Because the timing is right, I feel it behooves us to identify and move forward on the key issues and concerns regarding library service to homeschoolers. The number of home educators using libraries has increased significantly, with steady growth a good possibility. Therefore, it is more likely that concerns and new problems may crop up. For those reasons, I think each of us needs to seize the opportunity *now* to understand and accomplish at least some of the following:

1. study the real-life experiences/challenges colleagues have faced;

2. identify any homeschooling issues present in *our* libraries;

3. look at options and initiate practical solutions to the issues, relying on staff and homeschooler input;

4. ideally, to help manage change, build a coalition that includes home educators, school and public librarians, public school curriculum administrators, library board members and other citizens (form a structured advisory committee, if practical);

5. lead group discussions about homeschooling and educator issues, and follow through on suggestions;

6. update library board trustees on advisory committee proposals;

7. create a list of other potential "sticky" homeschooling issues.

Real-life concerns and experiences

The primary thrust of this chapter, the challenges relating to serving home educators in our libraries, is difficult to locate in library literature. In fact, with the exception of a few paragraphs in periodical articles and a brief mention in a recent professional book, it is nonexistent. Consequently, in this chapter I rely on my personal experiences and research, and commentary from colleagues. To gather current colleague information for this particular portion of the chapter, I mailed out hundreds of homeschooling surveys and posted messages with two large Internet discussion groups. Each survey contained a variety of questions about special services and programs, positive or negative experiences, and library policies (see appendix IX). Excerpts from these personal responses, in the form of quotations from librarians in ten states and Canada, make up one of the subsequent

parts of this chapter. These real-life challenges are numerous and diverse.

When filtered down, five main topics emerge:

• challenges with intent to censor

• challenges/objections with intent to just protest

• collection development issues

• providing curriculum vs. curriculum support

• interlibrary loan/borrowing privileges and policies.

Although not mentioned as frequently, librarians are concerned about a number of other related issues. (Please note: these examples may also pertain to any or all library users, not just home educators.)

Based on librarian experiences and my interpretations, recurring examples include:

• subject area depletion;

• reluctance to substitute curriculum materials/reliance on outdated, out-of-print booklists;

• frequently request "mountains" of materials that are needed "yesterday;"

• reluctance to use online catalog and similar service, or demand too much software/hardware/sophisticated computer access;

• unique programs/services offered to homeschoolers get no response;

• unsupervised homeschool children in the library.

The following comments also contain a variety of methods that may help guide you in the right direction. In some cases, the ideas and techniques are clearly spelled out. You will need to "read between the lines" with others. Some contain stereotypical statements that will be addressed later in the chapter. You may want to slowly sift through the anecdotes, looking for the prevalent issues or familiar threads mentioned earlier. Ultimately, these may help you find the best solutions to problems before they develop.

The following examples of concerns and cautions come from library colleagues around the country. These distinct reflections are based on personal experiences. (As before, the states are listed after each entry.)

- Often homeschooling parents had a list of books they had obtained from a mail order curriculum company or home school support group; the books were older titles from little known presses, so challenging ILL searches were a major part of reference work." (MA)

- No problems so far. We try to have Christian-oriented and secular books, so they know libraries represent all points of view. They also know they are ultimately responsible for what their children borrow, not the library staff. The local schools have had challenges, but we have not. We may see an increased demand/usage if voters outside the city limits approve a 'library district.' Currently, nonresidents pay a fee ($24 annually) to get a family library card, and there are undoubtedly homeschoolers who don't use the library for this reason. (WA)

- The only negative encounters have been their objection to our Halloween decorations (which are extensive and all over the library)." (MN)

- The potential of Christian homeschoolers raising censorship issues is always scary, but this means we should talk more now, before any problems arise." (MA)

- Most of our homeschoolers are very nice people but we have a few who have been so rude and demanding that the whole concept has taken on a bad aspect for us. These few demand that the policies be changed for them and keep insisting on special treatment. So far, fortunately, the staff members have remained calm and patient." (TN)

- I have had difficulty in trying to order materials for homeschoolers; for example, I don't know where to order Mary Pride's materials, and what I have requested of Raymond Moore's books are out-of-print. I have offered story-times and tours to homeschoolers, but so far they haven't accepted my offer." (IL)

- We do use ILL for out-of-date materials. We get what people ask for but often we have brand new beautiful books on the same subjects sitting on our shelves. We have also received requests for multiple copies of out-of-print books. Our only solution is to use ILL and let the patrons take turns." (TN)

- My only negative experience is with a particular home school father who left his three children unsupervised, one of whom is under three, in Youth Services for an extended period of time." (IL)

- The one negative experience occurred when a man who homeschools his son criticized library materials. He was offended that the library would purchase multicultural materials (in particular African folktales). He said he would never let his child use the library because the library housed materials that were not Christian-based. He further stated that all other ways of life were not worthy of learning." (MI)

- We certainly want to address their needs but need to keep in focus our primary mission. We are a public library, not a home or school library. The primary impact, if any, would be financial—if we spend staff time in teaching them how to use the library more intensively than we do for other customers, and if we invest materials budgets to purchase 'curricula' for them instead of our standard materials." (MN)

- I have received collection development suggestions that have helped. Mostly these were in the form of liking certain biography series, and couldn't we buy more? Also, I tried to initiate giving homeschoolers art display space, but they didn't take advantage of the opportunity." (IL)

"Of the challenges to books I have received over the past three years less than half came from homeschooling parents. However, the homeschooling parents would often express their views on books and I quickly learned which titles were not appropriate to recommend to them. For example, some of the families disapproved of picture books which contained animals dressed in clothing and speaking like humans. I also tended to recommend the books directly to the parents rather than the child as that seemed to be the way they preferred it." (MA)

"As far as collection development goes, a preponderance of materials dealing with Christian themes for homeschoolers would present problems for libraries trying to provide a balanced collection." (WI)

"Homeschoolers interests are more in nonfiction; they are, after all, thinking in terms of curriculum. I think it is fair to say that homeschooling parents are great supporters of, and usually appreciative of what libraries offer. They can thus be seen as useful advocates and perhaps even consultants on collection development." (Vancouver, B.C.)

"I have a problem with some homeschooling individuals who have their own sources for books, some very obscure, difficult to locate. I would provide curricula for home schoolers if it fell within our collection development policies." (WA)

"My collection development policy excludes textbooks, but I provide trade books on any topic. I figure if it is of interest to a homeschooler, it will be of interest to others. I take their recommendations for purchase seriously. They are educators and are treated as such. I have been dealing and working with homeschoolers for ten years and have never had a negative encounter." (PA)

"Some of our homeschooling families look for books off of outdated curricula lists. This includes severely outdated science materials." (IL)

"We do have copies of the local school district's curriculum goals and objectives by grade, and the state curriculum guidelines. We have various textbooks but do not buy grade-by-grade curriculum packages. People who use these generally want their own copies and do not expect the library to have them." (WA)

"Our collection is growing due to questions and concerns posted by homeschoolers. Many of the problems were simply due to lack of materials. We do not see home school curricula as important yet in the library. Thus far, our main concern is getting them to use our resources." (PA)

"Our library has cut back its extended privileges to public schools with the idea the public library is there to serve the individual child and family first. Our budget does not allow special collections either. We encourage homeschoolers to use the library like any teachers—as a supplemental, not primary source of materials. If our homeschooling population increased, we would allocate more resources. Like all public libraries, we have the difficult task of dividing limited resources among many service groups." (WI)

"In one instance, homeschoolers new to the area wanted significant numbers of books brought in from other libraries. The mother didn't want to pay the 25 cents per item request fee; thought it should be waived for homeschoolers. I explained she could do her own book searches and calls if she chose and there would be no fee." (WI)

"We would provide curricula to a certain extent. Our focus is that of a public library, not school library, and too much purchasing of curricula would rob our other users of their preferred materials. One homeschooler has stated they would like more attention given to teaching them how to use the library. I think they mean this as a school librarian would teach library skills to students.˝ (MN)

˝ Our main challenge is explaining why we don't have works that were published in the '50s and '60s that appear on their reading lists. Many of these works have been weeded from our collection a long time ago. Also, I have one patron who doesn't like the inconvenience of the interlibrary loan process.˝ (IL)

˝ We don't consciously buy curricular support materials, but do buy materials which can support juvenile learning. We suspect when we are online regionally they will make heavy use of ILL via our extension services. Telephone/modem/PC access to online library catalogs would be helpful if more of them had phones.˝ (MN)

˝ We do have curriculum guides from the public schools on file here. Schools get loans of six weeks; homeschoolers don't seem to need that much time. Also, the kids sometimes get left in the library while mom is off doing something else. Not a major problem though—we have latchkey school kids too! One of our library board members has homeschooled kids—I think he values us more now that he sees what we can provide.˝ (IL)

˝ Homeschooling is growing in our area, and we provide curriculum support, but no textbooks. We were unable to help one family that said they would need 10-12 books (specific titles) every week. That didn't fit with our three interlibrary loan requests per week rule.˝ (MN)

˝ Homeschoolers place great demands on our nonfiction collection. Adult Services seems to have more difficulty serving the teenaged homeschool population.˝ (IL)

˝ We have had to explain to some people that we may not have the exact title in American history (example) they want, but do have other books on their topics which would fulfill their needs and be available much faster than getting a specific title for them on interlibrary loan. Also, sometimes books are kept overdue.˝ (MN)

˝ One of the challenges in my estimation is that we simply don't have any written library policies and guidelines regarding service to homeschoolers. We certainly should be working to change that.˝ (WI)

˝ I don't mind providing some curricula, but we cannot provide enough to meet all their needs. I don't see homeschoolers making a particular impact. We have a strong collection for children and they are as welcome to make use of it as any other segment of the population.˝ (MN)

˝ We sometimes have difficulty providing desired support materials because the home schooling parent is unable to describe just what materials they need. Usually there are few problems.˝ (WI)

˝ My library board is concerned with not duplicating services that are available elsewhere. Therefore, we do not have school curricula or textbooks.˝ (IL)

˝ We do provide support for curricula. We do *not* provide curricular or lesson support for any educators—public, private, or home schools. Developing the planned program of lessons and courses is the responsibility of the educator, not librarians who have little training in the development of activities and lessons to bring about a desired learning outcome. We provide lessons in library use to teach specific skills, on request.˝ (WI)

˝ Right now homeschoolers have not asked for textbooks to be on hand at the library. We provide them with as much curriculum support/enrichment as we can. Homeschool teachers get extended loan periods, like all other teachers.˝ (IL)

˝ I'm not sure about curricula. I think schools should provide some materials for homeschooling families upon request. If there is a large body of homeschoolers who all want the same curriculum, I would think it may be appropriate for the library to have it. Libraries, especially in smaller communities, should be in touch with both the local school system and homeschool communities, to serve both their needs." (MA)

" Occasionally I felt conflicted when homeschoolers would request materials which I felt were out-of-date, incomplete, or otherwise inadequate. But they wanted those particular titles so I was restrained in pointing out weaknesses. Some examples were: a history book published in the 1940s, and a controversial, self-published AIDS book. Occasionally I offended them with what I did offer, especially in children's books, but I learned to scope out what they wanted, omit what they wouldn't approve of." (MA)

" One homeschooler last year told me the library was their best and favorite curriculum!" (MN)

" Our current batch of homeschoolers has an insatiable hunger for computer books and software, and asks tough questions about new technologies." (WI)

" We cannot provide all curriculum-related materials for home schoolers. Sometimes they ask for books we cannot supply." (IL)

" We have a discipline problem with homeschool children, when their parents are in the library meeting room. The kids are used to being allowed to run all around. I talked to them about this problem—it helped for a while. They want us to buy materials that fit their values; sometimes too fundamentalist. Also, they want materials through ILL quickly, and hand us lists of books they want. We need to train homeschoolers to be more self-sufficient, so they don't use up our time." (MN)

" Homeschoolers did demand a lot of ILL's but because of our policy of only allowing five ILL books per patron at a time this didn't become a problem. They also had a negative track record regarding the tons of children's books they checked out and didn't necessarily return on time. More and more demand for interlibrary loan it seems, and for media items." (MO)

" Homeschoolers who come on the bookmobile order videos and audios that are difficult to order through ILL because of the shorter loan period and my bookmobile schedule. Generally, they sure help my circulation numbers. I have also had parents ask me to remove a certain book from the collection." (MN)

Facing the questions and concerns

Now it's time to turn the puzzling questions and recurring patterns into sensible solutions. These ideas and solutions will hopefully encourage you to take action on some dormant homeschooling initiatives. If your library's involvement with homeschoolers is peripheral at best, perhaps you should apply these concepts to other library customers, leaving service to homeschoolers to the other "larger, financially healthy, robustly-staffed libraries." Unfortunately, I'm not sure how many libraries in the 1990s are able to lay claim to all three of those characteristics. My view, based on observation only, is that the "80/20 Rule" already adversely constrains library service to home educators. In other words, 80 percent of the work involved in serving home educators is being done by 20 percent of the librarians! (Or should that percentage be 95/5?)

One of the practical concerns aired more than once in colleague's responses relates to the use (or abuse) of *interlibrary loan services*. Since the number of people homeschooling their children has escalated in the last decade or two, with usage of libraries rising accordingly, this is a relatively new phenomenon. Specifically, librarians are now concerned that growing demands from homeschoolers will impact interlibrary loan patterns and services, with local and statewide ramifications. Keep in mind that this ILL matter is also interconnected with *curriculum issues*. The following recent examples should illustrate these points, and more.

In the Marigold Library System newsletter from Stathmore, Alberta, an article reported in 1994 that most member librarians, in response to a homeschooling survey, felt little impact from homeschoolers, but some were definitely concerned about a large increase in the use of their interlibrary loan service. (The article also mentions other concerns, including more demand for junior classic fiction and nonfiction, and teachers borrowing all the materials in one subject area.)

Jan Feye-Stukas of the Office for Library Development and Services (LDS), Minnesota Department of Education, sent a memorandum in 1993 to all regional public library systems, multi-type library agencies, and select other libraries about "Public School District Responsibilities for Providing Instructional Materials for Home Schools." The purpose of the memo was to clarify a section of the Minnesota Statutes for interlibrary loan librarians concerned about "the increasing demands from home schools for interlibrary loan service." Many librarians and library administrators were unaware that Minnesota public school districts are "required by law and rule, to offer, and if requested, provide textbooks, standardized tests, and individualized instructional materials for non-public students in their districts, including home school pupils." They also learned that school districts receive financial aid from the state of Minnesota for providing these specific services. Feye-Stukas, on behalf of the LDS staff, communicated that, "It is our understanding that home schools should obtain their primary instructional and educational materials from their local public school district offices and media

centers. Public library staff can help make these support services known to home school parents and teachers."[1]

This second example shows how interlibrary loan and curriculum issues are sometimes inseparable. It also indicates how librarians can act as resource people for homeschoolers. In my estimation, this is one of the critical roles we need to assume. Keeping the homeschooling resource file and ourselves up-to-date is very important. For instance, if we were familiar with state homeschooling laws and issues, we would realize that Minnesota's statutes are not consistent with homeschooling laws in other states. In fact, every state has unique home-based education statutes. In other words, many state laws don't provide for instructional or educational materials, or anything else, for homeschoolers. Conversely, a few states offer educational stipends to homeschooling families, through their public school districts, to be spent on curriculum materials. (Note: books that profile individual state home education laws are listed in the appendix/bibliography.)

On an informational handout designed for homeschool parents, the Wisconsin Department of Public Instruction (DPI) says, "Even though local school districts are not obligated to provide materials to home-based private educational programs, parents may contact their local school officials to determine if they can be of assistance. Other possible resources include bookstores or public libraries. DPI's role does not include providing curricular materials to parents for home-based private educational programs."[2] I am reminded of two "food for thought" realities.

First, because they receive financial aid for each pupil enrolled in their public schools, public school districts lose money when parents opt for the homeschool choice. Second, many homeschoolers are hesitant to be beholden to bureaucracies. Fearing state intervention in their home schools, they tend to ignore the "free" state services.

Considering all these factors, since Minnesota law names the school districts as responsible parties for providing some home school curriculum materials, can interlibrary loan librarians breathe a sigh of relief? In this specific case, or in general? In my opinion, the answer is—only in the case of not having to provide textbooks, standardized tests, graded curricula and similar materials. We still need to supply, as a number of colleagues mention, basic "curriculum support" materials for homeschoolers, and interlibrary loan services. *Curriculum support* could mean providing books on social studies, English, math or any other non-textbook materials that fit into the homeschooler's lesson or life plan. Librarians responding to my surveys were in alignment on this issue. They feel buying materials with homeschoolers in mind is fine, as long as some of the books, tapes, etc. are suitable for other library users as well. They also favor prudent use of the interlibrary loan network. Regarding ILL, I think following your general guidelines and policies is adequate, unless you have extraordinary limits and rules for educators. In all those cases, without exception, parents who homeschool should receive the same treatment as private and public school teachers. From my point of view, this is simply a question of fairness—what's good for one educator, is good for all educators.

Because of the financial constraints many libraries face, I feel adding a preponderance of homeschooling materials to all collections and allowing limitless ILL's is just not sensible. Instead, perhaps regional library systems could pick up some of the collection development "slack" by selecting pertinent homeschooling titles that would circulate on demand to their member libraries, and/or be shared throughout the state interlibrary loan system. Otherwise, as the hub of the library system wheel, designated "resource libraries" could be depositories for most

home education and curriculum support materials. For the convenience of the home-school customer though, smaller libraries should carry some homeschooling materials and have an adequate homeschool resource file.

Children's services and reference librarians from system headquarters or the resource library could produce detailed handouts, pathfinders and bibliographies. These would list, among other things, member libraries and their existing home-schooling resources. They would also assist librarians throughout the region, and would direct homeschoolers, who have been known to flit from library to library, to area libraries with good home education collections. To start the momentum rolling, I recommend having a systemwide meeting for whomever has an interest in library services to homeschoolers. Leaders, and a bunch of new ideas, will probably emerge from this meeting. At some later date, you may want to involve your homeschooling community and/or library volunteers in the project.

Other colleagues mention acquiring *curriculum guides* from local public school districts; these are perfect examples of items that should go in your homeschooling resource file. They afford curious home-schooling parents a glimpse of classes public schools are offering, and show step-by-step learning goals and objectives. Because most librarians are not trained to deal with sequential unit studies or curriculum matters, and don't understand the lingo, we need not masquerade as homeschool curriculum experts—thank goodness.

Many of us, however, need to be well versed in library *collection development*. Providing a balanced collection of materials, including ones that address certain viewpoints homeschoolers agree or disagree with, may mean purchasing controversial books on the occult, alternative lifestyles, sexuality, abortion, creation science/evolution, history and other subjects. When your materials selection program is in order, this is likely an ongoing process. Additionally, having procedures for handling complaints is imperative. An established public relations program and procedures for responding to censorship challenges is also a must. For further information on these, and related issues, consult the American Library Association's *Intellectual Freedom Manual*.[3] In my experience, allowing home educators to participate in materials selection is risky and wise. If you decide to do so, make sure to take opportunities to stress balanced collection, again and again. Communicate *your* feelings on a variety of issues. This candid sharing is very important because it builds trust. (In my opinion, would-be censors, and most library customers, will never understand why we are passionate about intellectual freedom and censorship. However, what you convey may mean a lot; in other words, your candor may silence the censor.) Also, take a moment to explain why reference and interlibrary loan librarians throw up their hands when presented a homeschooler list of history books from the twenties! Lastly, thank them for their suggestions regarding *KidsArt, Mothering, Parabola* or other magazines.

Two of the other questions I raised at the outset of this chapter deserve to be examined. Namely, do some librarians have an *attitude problem* about homeschooling, the people who elect to do it, and/or their ideology? If so, it is important to decide whether this bias is rooted in experience or stereotypes? Have actual conflicts, censorship challenges, policy fights, and other hassles soured your attitude, or are the opinions based on selected accounts and coverage in the media? If you, or people on your library staff, feel somewhat antagonistic toward homeschoolers, I think some honest self-examination may be in order. Otherwise, in my opinion, the scale of fairness becomes uneven. The second question relates to unsupervised children in the library. You may know more about this topic, especially if you're a children's librarian, than I ever will. However, if you don't, I'd suggest you read *Latchkey Children in the Library & Community: Issues, Strategies & Programs*, by Frances Dowd,[4] or an article entitled "Service to Latchkey Kids and the Public Library-Dealing with the Real Issues," by Linda Rome, which appeared in the April 1990 issue of *Wilson Library Bulletin*.[5] Best of luck to you!

Summary

This chapter acquainted you with issues and challenges librarians face when working alongside home educators in libraries. Without a doubt, all libraries and library systems are serving homeschoolers at a different level. Some are breaking trail, others haven't even found the woods yet. It should come as no surprise, considering the climbing statistics, that we are beginning to see more librarians focusing time and energy on preparing for homeschoolers in their library. A vital part of the "getting acquainted" process is for homeschoolers and librarians to openly discuss materials selection, intellectual freedom, balanced collections, censorship. Even though we may come from different orientations, we hopefully share a common pursuit—the love of learning and libraries. In my opinion, a fruitful partnership is a possibility, although there are some high hurdles to jump over first. Whenever I reread our colleagues' survey responses, I find myself pausing at the comment on how librarians should be in touch with both the public school and homeschooler communities. This gives rise to further questions—for instance, where do we go from here? Will we be able to manage change, including how new technologies influence libraries and (home) education? In the next chapter we will look ahead to the future, examining probable networking and interlibrary cooperation between public schools/school

A Guide to Homeschooling for Librarians

media centers, public libraries, regional library systems and homeschoolers.

Endnotes

1. Janice Feye-Stukas, to select Minnesota public library agencies, memorandum, 9 March 1993, "Public School District Responsibilities for Providing Instructional Materials for Home Schools," Office for Library Development and Services.

2. State of Wisconsin Department of Public Instruction, informational circular, Fall 1993, "Questions and DPI Responses Relating to Home-Based Private Educational Programs," p. 2.

3. Office for Intellectual Freedom, *Intellectual Freedom Manual*. Chicago: American Library Association, 1992.

4. Dowd, Frances. *Latchkey Children In the Library & Community: Issues, Strategies & Programs*. Phoenix, Oryx Press, 1991.

5. Rome, Linda. "Service to Latchkey Kids and the Public Library—Dealing with the Real Issues." *Wilson Library Bulletin*, (April 1990): 34-37, 126.

4

Envisioning the Future
Cooperation and Connections

The library of the future "will be full of computers and there will be robots for librarians," according to one young participant at a planning retreat sponsored by the Montgomery County (Maryland) Department of Public Libraries. During this 1994 strategic planning process, twenty children and young people, from fourth to eleventh grade (including one home-schooler), projected their feelings about what libraries would be like at the start of the new millennium. They were asked three key questions: 1) What will you use libraries for in the year 2000? 2) What will libraries look like in the year 2000? 3) What would you like at the library today that you did not find? Their creative minds generated dozens of unique ideas. They felt the library would be a meeting place where a variety of people from the community came to learn and interact. Some kids saw librarians in a central location being called upon to assist in the use of interactive television (especially those not already replaced by robots). Security issues would be extremely important because of the huge numbers of computers in libraries. Environmental preservation was an oft-mentioned concern; they felt using the library's resources via home computer would be a way to reduce

pollution caused by automobiles. The amount of paper consumed to make books and other materials was brought up, the destruction of forests being their main concern. In the future, libraries would need print copies as backups to the electronic ones. Some "with it" young adults saw libraries with many computers hooked into wide area and local networks, and computers for writing projects and online information access. Others felt there should even be a room for virtual reality activities.[1]

Clear and original ideas—from the minds of young brainstormers! Libraries have much to look forward to, according to these visionaries. When boiled down, two themes spring forth from their predictions. The years ahead will bring: A) dramatic technological changes, and B) more opportunities to make human and technological connections. These two themes, and the notion of compromise and cooperation, appear consistently throughout this chapter.

Although I am a resolute advocate of technological changes in almost all cases, and especially when they benefit libraries and library customers, I don't like the idea of a robot replacing me at the Waukesha Public

Library! Though I may playfully scoff at the idea of robots performing my various job functions, as *you* might be inclined to, the truth is that I am much less skeptical than I used to be. These days, the amazing seems so possible. With the help of a global computer network, I instantaneously chat with Uncle Reidar in Norway, dial into a remote academic library site in Miami, or trade research ideas with a friend and colleague in Missoula, Montana, interested in home education issues. Thirty years ago I never would have imagined, even in my wildest youthful dreams, that having a computer and modem would give me access to the world. Consequently, in the 1980s and 1990s, mainly due to technological advancements and networking, improbabilities have become realities.

Whether we acknowledge it or not, technology is speeding along like a rocket on an inexorable path to the future. Libraries are riding that rocket, changing and adapting as necessary. Library collections are expanding and decreasing in different ways. Big, visible, vinyl phonodiscs are being phased out, making room for small, shiny CD-ROM products that "disappear" inside multimedia home computers. Twenty-foot-long reference sets are now available on two 4$\frac{1}{2}$" compact discs. Services and programs are also quickly evolving with the technological times. Electronic bulletin boards are speeding up the interlibrary loan process. Remote computer access to a variety of library collections allows library customers to look around the region for materials they need, and reserve them from home if they so desire, saving a trip to the library building. (One library user of dial-in access, encouraging me to link up, enthusiastically stated, "It's almost like having the whole library in your den!") In some cases, a small white dish bolted to the library rooftop captures signals from a skyborne satellite, instantly relaying a continuing education course to a community classroom in the library. Using that same communication linkup, library

"information services" staff actively participate in an international teleconference on computer virus and network security issues. (Look for more on this "distance learning" phenomena later in this chapter.) The list of examples goes on and on. No doubt about it—the future has rocketed into our libraries and is here to stay!

Coming down to earth again, we face an important question: 1) how much time, energy and money should an individual library or library system invest in technology, and how does that pertain to serving homeschoolers? (This echoes a previous question—how much should your library invest in serving home educators?) In my opinion, libraries should get on the technology track as soon as possible, for the benefit of all library users. We should not necessarily follow the identical technology path other libraries have taken; instead, jumping aboard with some innovative ideas, at a time when our financial and staffing realities encourage risk taking, may be a creative *and* safe move.

Keeping all that in mind, I finally need to mention that in this particular chapter we will investigate: 1) the library's future role in community learning, distance education, computer networks, and provision of technology-related resources, 2) networking and cooperation possibilities between libraries, and public, parochial, private and home schools, 3) the onset of online home schooling, 4) new educational choices and trends, 5) the fantastic future, and 6) how library service to homeschoolers and other customers could expand and/or change, due to imminent or existing technologies. Additionally, I will feature some real-life examples of public school and homeschool partnerships, and pose some "challenge questions" about the future of library service to homeschoolers.

The library as homeschool laboratory

Libraries are to homeschoolers what brick and mortar school buildings are to public school students. They are free (taxpayer supported), useful, multipurpose facilities. Libraries act as reading and research rooms, study halls, media and computer training centers, meeting places, and entertainment sites. To homeschoolers, libraries are convenient classrooms, a change of pace from their home space. In essence, libraries are like "general learning laboratories," places that encourage observation and experimentation. These laboratories commonly stock an enormous variety of educational and recreational materials, in scores of different formats. Whenever financially possible, they provide online catalogs, personal use computers, CD-ROM databases and/or other cutting edge technologies for their customers.

According to the survey responses I mentioned in chapter two, and other verbal queries, homeschoolers are eager to sample the new technologies. They want their children to be proficient computer users. They also see the potential of incorporating this knowledge, and online competency, into their homeschool curriculum. For many home educators, computers are like electronic building blocks—an important first step in the lifelong educational process. Knowing this, is it time we planned, budgeted, and purchased more new technologies for homeschoolers, and other devout library customers? Should we actively reach out to the community of home educators, offering regular hands-on classes and tours profiling the current technology? Is it time, after careful study, to get rid of some of the outdated print formats? Essentially, are we ready for a metamorphosis—one where we turn into the "high-tech laboratory"—without sloughing off the "general learning laboratory" skin? From a risk-taking, progressive, "let's get ready for the future because it's already

here" point of view, the answers are emphatically yes. Many homeschoolers and other library advocates are calling for a transformation; they realize when libraries jump on the fast moving technology train, all customers will benefit. In the end, everyone's learning curve will expand.

If *your* library staff and management are ready to assess the library's current technology situation and seem willing to explore alternatives, you may want to look over my "recipe" of ideas listed below. Some pertain to homeschoolers, others to all library users. I freely admit many of these are idealistic ingredients, contingent upon available space, money, and expertise. You may already be one of the fortunate ones, offering a number of these technological advances at your library. Some of these may actually be services and programs you thought improbable or even impossible, yet somehow they were implemented. (It's strange how that regularly happens.) One word of caution—some of these "recipe ingredients" may lead to large expenditures, and, like with gifts of licorice to a child, may lead to increasing demands for more and better offerings!

"Recipe" for creating your high-tech laboratory

- A private room for video or laserdisc screenings and production equipment;
- New display devices, such as high-definition television;
- Multimedia computers for children, young people and adults;
- CD-ROM software packages, including electronic encyclopedias;
- An easy-to-use online computer system with simple, graphic tutorials;
- Public access to remote pay-per-use databases (DIALOG, MEDLINE, etc.);
- Capability to place reserves online (in library) and by dial-up access;

- A public terminal that allows customers to do their own interlibrary loans;
- One self-checkout station for every 2,000 daily circulations;
- Numerous personal computers (all makes) for public/homeschooler use;
- Computers linked up to local, regional and global bulletin boards;
- Inexpensive full Internet access and regular Internet how-to classes;
- State statutes of all fifty states on CD-ROM (for home education laws);
- TDD/TTY machines, text telephones, other assistive learning tools;
- CD-ROM databases covering a variety of subjects, including education;
- Public telefacsimile and faxmodem services offered at reasonable costs;
- Hardware, software and modems available for long or short-term loan;
- Computers that access online curricula/real-time classes and offer computer-mediated instruction;
- Interactive educational software for special needs children of all ages;
- Current pathfinders on homeschool Usenet Newsgroups, etc.;
- In-house satellite dish to downlink educational programs/classes;
- Connection to a fiber optic network that links K-12 and other schools;
- An active, working partnership with your community free-net.

Note: Unlike most recipes, it is not necessary to mix and blend all these ingredients; simply choose the most affordable options that suit your needs and customers' desires.

Many home educators and their children will visit the technology-rich public library to study, do electronic research, connect with colleagues, take classes and supplement their lifelong learning. In the future, while they may primarily use the library to learn about new technologies, homeschool families will also give back to libraries by actively volunteering, suggesting book or media titles, helping as literacy (and technology) tutors, storytelling in the children's room, and helping with fund raisers. To show our appreciation and to foster cooperation, we should encourage interested homeschooled kids to become apprentices in the library.

Future cooperation

The key word in the subtitle of this chapter is cooperation. I feel we must come up with fresh and practical approaches for cooperation between libraries/homeschoolers/school districts, and reexamine our ideas regarding who plays what role. We need to test some new models in the wind tunnel. It's difficult to envision a positive future for library service to homeschoolers without teamwork and innovation. In my opinion, we need a concerted, grassroots effort. As soon as possible, we need to round up the following people, in each and every community, put them in a quiet room and let them talk: public school library/media center coordinators, school curriculum administrators, public librarians, private school librarians, library system librarians (not just children's services coordinators) and of course, homeschooling parents. They need to chat and argue about teaching and learning methods, homeschool stereotypes, public and alternative schools, curriculum issues, communal resources, the importance of libraries and library funding, their technological future, the inevitability of the virtual library, and other concerns. Only then can we expect the cooperative ball to start rolling.

Once the momentum of collaboration is in motion, the group will collectively decide how to work together, opening up some opportunities for each other and home educators, through better resource sharing/cost effective interlibrary loan (ILL), joint continuing education, cooperative collection development, shared local area computer networks (LANs), grantwriting partnerships, and online and CD-ROM database technologies. This give and take should occur without anyone making lopsided sacrifices. Before we make changes we should also remember to stress the educational needs of children—what are *their* wishes and dreams—should they even be part of this new, cooperative process, like the visionary Montgomery County youngsters were?

Hopefully, as a direct result of this process, school librarians will eventually be more willing to open their collections to home educators, with some limits, and school curriculum experts will share samples of their curricula with public librarians, who in turn will share with home educators. Homeschoolers will learn about the school district's policies on home education, and meet people who choose the school curriculum materials. Ideally, they will come away with a new perspective and willingness to volunteer at their community library and/or get involved in the public schools (I will cite examples of volunteer tutoring later in this chapter, when I talk about home school/public school cooperation). Library system people and state library leaders will finally support decentralized, grassroots multitypes that are compact, community-centered, and electronically-connected, and that work more efficiently than widespread, multi-county library organizations.

Public, private and school librarians will discover that sharing resources through cooperative ILL and collection development makes sense, especially considering the budgetary realities and limitations that most municipalities, counties and states are facing. In many public and private schools, librarians fight a constant battle to retain or increase funds for their library/media centers; when funding gets tight, school library/media center budgets often get sliced first, and not just in California. Public libraries funded by municipalities and counties, when compared to

other departments such as police, fire, and public works, frequently end up holding the short end of the budget stick. In the future, library systems and even state library agencies will be affected by this scarcity issue, unless they build alliances and networks, fight for their finances, and foster collaboration. If this happens, a best case scenario may arise, where people on governing boards view paving the information superhighway as crucial as paving the airport runway.

Due to recent technological advancements, public libraries are becoming satellite downlink sites/teleconference centers for the general public and library community. Public libraries have a long history of providing: 1) learning space for extended campus education, 2) test proctoring, 3) humanities programming, and 4) public meeting rooms for community use. I think this new satellite technology has the potential to greatly expand these options, making hundreds of remote classes and other opportunities readily available. In the near future, it is likely public libraries and/or library systems, acting on behalf of the area's multitype librarians and home educators, will organize and host more free teleconferences focusing on education issues. Unique topics will include: public school trends, home and alternative education, school choice, educational and library funding, continuing education, censorship, curriculum choices, technology in public and school libraries, and the emergence of virtual schools and libraries. When looking into the future, I feel these questions need to be addressed: 1) Where will people connect with these, and other technologies? 2) Will those connections be readily available and vigorously promoted at the public library?

This interactive teleconferencing will greatly expand learning choices for homeschoolers living in remote areas. Additionally, it will become a key feature of the homeschool laboratory, enabling home educators in different regions to stay connected. For homeschoolers and others, satellite dishes will be a popular way to access the global educational world. (Another way, online home schooling, will be discussed later in this chapter.) For a nominal fee, libraries will "beam in" educational experts, homeschool leaders from around the country, teachers, futurists, library educators, and other noteworthy presenters. Depending upon how fast this distance education develops, it is likely home educators will soon be able to listen and participate in national and statewide homeschooling conferences. Regional and/ or state home education support groups, partnering with library continuing education and technology people, will co-sponsor satellite continuing education classes at downlink library sites. (In areas where library schools are not plentiful, libraries will be vital teleducation connection sites for students accumulating credits toward their MLS or Library/Media Education degrees.) *In the future, for home-schoolers and all other library customers, it's critical that libraries provide connection points to these technologies at the library!*

Applying more technology to learning is a positive, logical step in the right direction, but this teleconferencing concept is not for everyone. However, as a complement to other technologies, the addition of a satellite dish on your library rooftop may reap huge benefits for homeschoolers, librarians and teachers, and help mobilize the educational community. (You may prefer other types of distance learning, such as computer conferencing and teleclasses.) In my view, all these ideas are worth pursuing. They are especially practical if your local library board has underscored "Community Education" as one of your three or four primary roles.

Current technology enables groups (like the collaborative one I propose in this chapter) to quickly interact and achieve their goals. They can write, discuss and revise their plans from afar, using network word

processing technology and video conferencing. Toward the end of this chapter, I will share more ideas about the future and its technological impact on libraries. For now, let's look at the new future of home-schooling—the emergence of online education. Knowing more about this topic will prepare librarians for an impending *new* role—that of providers of Internet access to the general public, including homeschoolers.

The onset of online home education

For homeschoolers with high-powered computers, a telephone line and a modem, the future has arrived. Dialing in from their home computers, homeschooled children and their parents can access a whole new world of information, trade ideas with fellow home educators, chat with electronic penpals in another state (or on another continent), download educational software and books from remote file servers, browse around thousands of library catalogs, and even capture homeschooling coursework from Internet files.

Although most home educators still teach in fairly traditional ways, using homemade or correspondence curricula, many are beginning to discover the benefits of using multimedia software and/or online information in their daily teaching routine. Using encyclopedic multimedia software like Encarta, homeschool children do unit studies on segments of history, geology, literature, people, religion and more, in their home or at the library. Progressive, profit motivated companies, aiming directly at the electronic homeschooler niche, are busily marketing individual CD-ROMs on the Bible, Shakespeare, psychology, science, math, English and world geography. Additionally, the large online companies that charge monthly fees and usage surcharges are very popular with homeschooling parents.

It is their ability to connect with a confederation of computers, such as the fabulously popular Internet, that appeals most to technologically adept home educators. Technology-based schooling is attractive to home educators for a variety of reasons. Bruce Nelson, the father of five home-schooled kids, says, "We have gotten ideas for science projects from the Internet, shared ideas with others via Prodigy and CompuServe and will give more emphasis to interactive collaboration for our kids later this year through Internet links." A marketing executive at Novell, the network software corporation, Nelson "is working with the local cable television company to create a network that includes access to interactive educational software and the Internet." In another corner of the country, eleven-year-old Rachel Loss-Cutler, who is homeschooled with her younger sister Ariana, answers online mythology quiz questions. Rachel also logs onto the Internet "to get Academy One, an educational service that offers classroom discussions and resources." Her father, Ken Loss-Cutler, is "president of the North Texas Free-Net, a nascent community network that offers free access to the Internet." He is also "in charge of the parent's section of Academy One, a 'virtual classroom' hosted by the National Public Telecomputing Network," and a sysop (systems operator) of the homeschooling section of CompuServe's education forum, a focal point for many homeschoolers seeking advice from veterans."[2]

For home educators willing to supplement their normal print curriculum with an electronic version, the "Imsatt Corp. of Falls Church, Virginia, in concert with the Calvert School of Baltimore, and other universities, is offering an online curriculum named Homer, via CompuServe or the Internet. Using Homer, students can study and be tested on nearly any subject imaginable, but the connection fees add up, at $3 to $6 per hour."[3] The Oak Meadow School, a nonreligious curriculum provider based in Blacksburg, Virginia, also encourages homeschoolers to utilize its

online capabilities to speed up coursework and grading. In Ionia, Michigan, a controversial log home charter school, the Noah Webster Academy, is linked up with its 2,000 cyberstudents via a shared computer network.[4]

Although some experts feel that online homeschooling will meet with minimal success and few converts, there are others who firmly believe that technology will dramatically transform homeschooling. Teaching children on computer networks is a radical departure from traditional styles of homeschooling. For that reason, parents who are techno-savvy, seeking alternatives to public or private schools, may be tempted by the "virtual homeschooling" option. They are also attracted to the idea of creating voluntary electronic links with their friends, homeschool colleagues, and support groups. According to homeschoolers I've talked with, children welcome the challenge and change of online education. It links them with new penpals (or should they *now* be called cyberpals?) and creates a huge, new classroom without walls. Students who were once fairly content learning alongside their brothers and sisters, now want to communicate with other homeschooled kids around the country. New, ever-broadening technologies and connections make that possible.

If home educators have no access to computers with modems at home, for whatever reason, where will they go to connect? If they wish to study fresh water mammals, how machines work, or take a simulated walk in outer space, using multimedia software and hardware they don't have at home, where will they go to connect? Where will the communication links be? Will they be available at a post office kiosk, in the YMCA, in the supermarket, at the chamber of commerce, or at the local library? In my opinion, the timing is right for librarians to take action. Libraries have a great opportunity to take the lead, to race ahead of others in providing Internet access to the entire public, including public school students, not just homeschool customers who tap into it for educational purposes. In the future, stand alone databases and satellite dishes will come and go, like itinerant tight ends in football. (They can't help it if they're just big receivers, waiting for their monthly floppy disk upgrade or a signal to catch.) On the other hand, because of its infinite digital loop and connectivity possibilities, the Internet is one of the keys to the future. Schools, homeschools and libraries of all types need to get connected, so they can foster communication and cooperation.

The homeschool/public school connection

The relationship between home educators and public school teachers and administrators is evolving; only Pollyanna would claim things have always been rosy. The truth is, the relationship has been contentious for years. Disagreements are plentiful and deep-rooted. Some of the issues relate to: competition, finances, teacher certification, collective bargaining, homeschooler participation in extracurricular activities, standardized testing, centralization vs. decentralization, truancy, compulsory education laws, school reentry, and homeschooler stereotyping. There are numerous signs, however, that changes in attitude and tolerance are on the horizon. The following examples foreshadow a truce between home schools and public schools. They also bode well for my optimistic ideas and predictions about future cooperation between people in various libraries, and public, private and home schools.

According to Jo Anna Natale, writing in the *American School Board Journal*, the bristly attitudes that public school officials and homeschoolers often show toward each other are slowly changing. She comments that, "public school officials realize they gain little by alienating the homeschool population, and as homeschoolers realize they can reap benefits from public schools,

hard lines seem to be softening a bit." In a concluding opinion Natale says, "As advocates of public education, school board members and administrators might not agree with parents' decisions to educate their children at home. But friction often makes matters worse. There's no guarantee a homeschooling parent will want a school district's help, but there are advantages for schools in finding ways to keep the communication lines open." In that same article, John Marshall, director of legislative services for the Oregon School Boards Association reflects, "We are becoming relatively tolerant of homeschoolers. The idea is, let's give the kids access to public schools so they'll see it's not as terrible as they've been told, and they'll want to come back."[5]

In an article entitled, "Home Schooling a Legitimate Alternative," Joyce El-Amin, a Beloit (Wisconsin) public school teacher, addresses her colleagues in a statewide publication, affirming that, "Home schoolers are not out to destroy the public schools and the good that they offer. They want the freedom to decide the course of their children's education. These parents do not think they are necessarily better teachers than public school teachers, rather they feel that teachers simply have too many students to be effective."[6] Free-lance writer and homeschooling parent Stephanie Wilson, writing in *Instructor* magazine, points out that, "Misconceptions about homeschooling abound, including some commonly held by homeschooling parents themselves." She goes on to say, "The skills needed to teach one's own children are not the same skills needed for classroom teaching; parents teaching at home don't need all the lesson plans, materials, and techniques that are important in the classroom." In the spirit of clarification, she asserts that comparatively few people choose homeschooling "in response to a bad experience with a school system."[7]

Citing evidence of positive relationships between homeschoolers and public school officials, doctoral candidate Celia Bishop, in her 1991 dissertation, mentions how certain homeschool support group members were invited to speak at a local college about their chosen educational alternative. The room was full of school administrators. Although the home-schoolers "were scared to death" about the opportunity, they discovered the public school people were very congenial and mainly curious about curriculum materials, publishers, and homeschool teaching methods. One of Bishop's survey respondent's claimed, "There are a lot of individuals in the public school system who are sympathetic to the home schooling movement because they are educators first. They believe in teaching. They delight in the imparting of knowledge to children. And when they see a system that works, they are enthusiastic about it." Another respondent related that, "My son has a learning disability. And one of the public school teachers, believe it or not, said what he needs is one-on-one for awhile. I said, how do you get one-on-one? Are you talking about home schooling? And she said, yeah, off the record, that is kinda what I am talking about. If you can't get it in the public school, you are going to have to get it through a tutor, or do it yourself."

In the conclusion to her doctoral disser-tation, Celia Bishop recommends changes in administrator and teacher training programs at universities and colleges. She also calls for increasing awareness of home education for all public school officials. Bishop believes, "To prepare public school teachers and administrators to make informed decisions regarding the home-schooling movement, teacher training insti-tutions should make provision in their curriculum for specific information regarding the homeschooling movement, its legal implications, and its future in American education." Higher education should offer home schooling parents, "workshops, training sessions, and continuing education services for the

purpose of instructing the teaching parent on educational methodologies and child development stages, with application directed toward the tutorial environment." She says, "It is recommended that public school authorities become aware of the functions of the homeschooling movement by reading its variety of publications which explain the aims and goals of the movement, its academic and social outcomes, its legal status, the aspirations and expectations of teaching parents, and the role of the homeschooling parent support groups in the local communities. It is also recommended that public school authorities work with the local home-schooling parent support group to serve as conduits for information to assist families interested in homeschooling their children. Homeschooling students should be encouraged to avail themselves of public school facilities that the homeschooling family cannot duplicate because of expense, expertise, or group necessity. Courses such as band, choir, theater, sports, and laboratory science should be made available."[8]

In a University of Maine, College of Education research report entitled, "Home-schooling: Issues for Administrators," authors Denise Mirochnik and Walter McIntyre boldly raise the issues of accep-tance, collaboration and cooperation, and children's rights. In their conclusion they emphasize that:

- "State department personnel, local school officials and parents need to find ways to work together to arrive at the best possible programs for home-schooled children, and respect home-schooling as a viable alternative to formal schooling.

- Perhaps children should have some say in where they want to be schooled.

- It is important that the homeschooled family not be isolated from the community school and its members and activities nor the community school isolated from homeschooling members and activities.

- Representatives from homeschooling organizations need to be consulted and recognized as important members of the educational community.

- Public colleges and universities need to make service and training available to homeschooling organizations and family networks.

- Conversely, homeschooling families need to establish working relationships with local school officials and be open to requests for information and other data which help shape educational policy and planning.

- Providing the opportunity for home education students to participate in local schools could help to create a new concept of what constitutes 'public education,' by acknowledging the need to recognize parents' contributions to their children's education.

- We are ultimately talking about the lives of children—how they are socialized, how they grow and develop—and the responsibilities we, as adults—parents and educators—have in providing the best possible future for children."[9]

Teacher, writer and educational reformer John Holt felt that, "schools have as much to gain by supporting home schoolers as they have to lose by opposing them." In a 1983 *Phi Delta Kappan* article he hoped schools would "hasten to set their feet on the path to cooperation." In this article entitled, "Schools and Home Schoolers: A Fruitful Partnership," Holt profiles the experiences of the Mahoney family of Barnstable, Massachusetts. The two children and their mother (the girls' primary teacher) are fortunate because their local school system is very cooperative. In the words of Holt, the school board invited the "children to use the schools, and their staff members and equipment, as part of their learning resources. In other words, the

Mahoney girls could come to school as part-time volunteers, to use the library or take a special class, to go on a field trip, use a lab or shop, or take part in such activities as music, drama, and sports. This pattern of cooperation between schools and what we have come to call homeschoolers exists in a small but increasing number of school districts in different parts of the U.S." Holt clarified this by saying, "Although such patterns of cooperation are occurring more frequently, they still seem to be more the exception than the rule. Most school districts, faced with a family that wishes to teach its own children, tend to respond with grudging tolerance."

John Holt cites a number of reasons why the public schools should cooperate with home educators, including the following:

- "Cooperation might bring the schools good publicity, and that would be a welcome change.

- Cooperation is likely to yield important ideas and methods that might help schools solve many of their most serious and intractable problems.

- Home schoolers using the school facilities will bring in considerable energy, enthusiasm, independence, intelligence, self-motivation, and a wide range of interests.

- Some home schoolers may be interested in working as aides to teachers of younger children. They could relieve teachers of routine tasks, such as reading to the class, which, though dull for teachers, would not seem dull to young volunteers."

He also explains his, "model home-schooling law," which he felt, once enacted, had the potential to "remove one of the major obstacles to full cooperation between schools and homeschooling families." The obstacle he refers to here is financial aid to public school districts. According to Holt, and others, "one reason superintendents have been unwilling to allow families to teach their own children is that they fear—and often say candidly—that the schools will lose financial aid."[10]

Mike Shepherd, a bilingual teacher at the Reinhardt Elementary School in the Dallas Independent School District, recently wrote an article about a home school/public school collaboration—"Home Schoolers As Public School Tutors." For two years he coordinated a program in which teenage homeschoolers volunteered in his public elementary school class. Joe, a seventeen-year-old homeschooler, tutored students in writing and reading, created classroom posters to supplement novels the class was reading, and helped with language arts and social studies. It turned out to be a good reprieve for Joe—a welcome break from his homeschool routine—and the public school students enjoyed the new experience. The second year, a thirteen-year-old homeschooler named Mike helped by grading papers and assisting with special projects. In the opinion of Mike Shepherd, "At a time when many schools are hurting for volunteers, homeschoolers in the community should not be ignored. Why not agree to disagree on some sensitive issues and pool our resources in areas on which we can agree? Parents who choose to school their children at home can benefit from the schools, and the schools can benefit from their presence in the following ways:

- Older homeschooled students can tutor public elementary students.
- Older homeschoolers can teach mini-courses in art or other specialties.
- Homeschoolers can attend music classes offered at the public schools and pay any fees necessary.
- Home-taught students can enroll in school but use the school's curriculum for home study.
- Schools can test home-taught students using nationally normed tests.

- Home-taught kids can be allowed to compete in science fairs and spelling bees along with public school students.
- Home-taught kids can be invited to special school events and field trips."

Shepherd is emphatic that, "Children must not lose out because no one is willing to meet the parents halfway." After his two-year tutoring experience, he is convinced further cooperation is possible, saying, "We must leave the public school doors open wide for all kids."[11]

Examples of school systems that open their doors and services to home educators are now easier to find than they were in John Holt's time—when he wrote his 1983 article about homeschool/public school partnerships, home education was still not legal in *all* fifty states, as it is in 1995. Still, in 1995, some schools take a strong prohibitive stance with homeschoolers, preferring a "closed door" to an "open door" policy. However, as the preceding and following examples show, a new trend is slowly and steadily emerging—school districts are beginning to collaborate with home educators. One such system is the Bennett Valley School District in Santa Rosa, California. Worried about declining enrollment (partially due to home educators leaving for less restrictive school districts), and the loss of state tax dollars, Bennett Valley created a plan that actively supported homeschoolers. Their new program essentially reimbursed homeschooling parents up to $1,000 per child per year, to be used for curriculum materials, field trips, and more. The school district also allowed homeschoolers to utilize the school library, attend photo and health examination days, and participate in extracurricular activities. The project had been quite successful. Three years ago twenty-two children enrolled; in 1994, approximately 250 K-6 youngsters participated. Presently, due to recent State Department Of Education intervention, the program is no longer available to homeschoolers in the Bennett

Valley School District, or anywhere in California.

Probably the most famous model of homeschool/public school cooperation (and homeschool subsidization) comes out of California's "Silicon Valley," from the Cupertino School District. Their trailblazing independent study program was profiled in a *Wall Street Journal* feature story.[12] What was unique about Cupertino's program was that a family didn't need to live there to participate. Subsidies were doled out to parents, $1,000 per child, to be used for products and services such as those available to school students. These could include: field trips, art supplies, foreign language tapes, books, computer software and more. Religious curriculum items were not reimbursed. Principal Frank Clark, administrator of the Cupertino independent study initiative, referred to the program as a win-win situation for both schools and families. He began to see homeschooling parents in a more positive light, and was sure homeschoolers would be more likely to choose the Cupertino schools when their teenagers were ready to return to a conventional public school setting. Programs like these stimulated schools to be competitive, in Clark's opinion.

Another example of this experimental collaboration thrives in the Midwest, where in Ames, Iowa, the Community School District's Home-Based Education Program is making headlines. Under the Iowa "dual enrollment" bill, homeschoolers can legally "enroll in their school district for academic or instructional programs, participate in extracurricular activities, or use the services and assistance offered by the appropriate area educational agency. What that means for families and school districts is that home education can be a team effort in alternative education." According to homeschooler Mary Terpstra, Coordinator of the Home-Based Education Program, "taking the team approach has real benefits for the public school system. In Iowa, the

school district can receive state aid for those homeschooled children who choose to be part of their school community. Even more important, home educators who feel connected to their schools will support those schools more fully—and support of the community is critical to public schools. Home educators in our area attend school functions and feel they are a part of our Ames School District. We even have home educating parents who volunteer in classrooms. We all recognize that our goal is to help each child reach his or her educational goals."[13]

A good example of cooperation *and* the utilization of technology to connect public schools and home educators is happening in Arizona. A "customized tutorial" program allows homeschoolers to tap into a school teacher's expertise for difficult subjects such as the pure sciences and mathematics. The public schools benefit by retaining their state funding for all homeschoolers enrolled in the new program. The future plan is to have a remote access option where home educators and/or their children can dial into a school district's computer for coursework and other information.

School districts are not the only ones changing their tune about home schoolers. Arnold Fege, Director of Federal Relations for the national Parent Teacher Association (PTA), is concerned about boosting the cooperation and candor between the two groups. He asks, "Why isn't it possible for kids to come to school in the morning and take advantage of social studies-type things, and then have parents teach them in the afternoon? It would be a rich education, and it would help cement relations between the home and school as an equal partnership."[14] Also, well-known homeschool researcher J. Gary Knowles from the University of Michigan says he, "would hope the school system is changing to be more responsive to individuals, and that schools all over the nation begin to accept parents as a really important part of the system."[15]

Other innovative examples of collaboration and sharing are happening around the country, including, but certainly not limited to the following:

- In Minneapolis, Minnesota, homeschoolers romp together at a community recreation center. New collaborative programs encourage homeschoolers to use various school services, including gyms and libraries. Public school/home-school liaison Tom Murray says the school system has no policies restricting home educators. He describes the cooperative relationship as open, trusting, nurturing.

- In San Diego, California, the Community Home Education Office boasts six full-time teachers who work with nearly 200 homeschooled students.

- The movement is so established in West Virginia that the state legislature sponsors an annual "homeschoolers day." Homeschoolers serve as pages while their parents discuss pertinent issues with lawmakers.

Public school administrators, burdened with financial concerns, lack of clear legal precedent, and the turmoil of change, continue to wrestle with a plethora of homeschooling issues. According to Kathy Collins, legal counsel to the Iowa Department of Education, writing in *The School Administrator*, a middle ground needs to be found. Perpetuating the long-standing home school/public school battle would be very damaging to school districts, Collins claims. She is convinced, "The opportunity is there for school administrators to make the public schools look like the most open-minded and accepting of alternatives just by the way they treat homeschooling families. But the potential is greater for a public relations nightmare, for an administrator to be caught in an inflexible position, to be involved in a lawsuit or to have some parents take the whole thing to the media." The middle ground, or compromise that she refers to is the Iowa "dual enrollment" option. As mentioned in the earlier Ames, Iowa example, when homeschooling students enroll in the public schools under this plan, the schools don't lose state financial aid. Kathy Collins feels "the liberalization of laws may force a compromise between two groups at polar extremes from each other— the public schools who believe they can meet all the needs of the child, which is frankly folly, and homeschoolers who mistakenly believe they can provide everything at home for the child." When summing up the entire situation, she concludes that, "In the end, it's up to school administrators to decide."[16]

Fostering cooperation

Relationships have definitely improved between homeschoolers and school officials. Innovative, collaborative programs are well underway. Compromises are being struck in all regions of the country. Home-school children, once considered truants, are now tutoring in some public schools. Homeschool parents are enrolling their kids in extracurricular programs and utilizing public school teacher expertise. Nevertheless, cooperation is not universal. Relationships between homeschoolers and public school administrators needs to consistently improve. I admit it's a bit idealistic to expect people with opposing viewpoints to agree on major educational issues. Because of the size of the philosophical gap, instant cooperation is unrealistic. However, I believe if everyone focuses more on what's best for children, de-emphasizing financial, competitive and territorial concerns, they can steadily chip away at the old paradigm and speed up collaboration. Librarians could play a pioneering role in this scenario.

Perhaps one way *we* could foster cooperation is by facilitating public dialogue about education issues at public libraries, in the form of panel discussions, debates or conferences. Forget the aforementioned satellite or video conferencing technology—just open up the large library meeting room for lively debate about public and home education. Librarians could even be moderators of the sessions. (Since there's "no love lost" between some homeschoolers and school officials/school teachers, the moderator must be impartial and experienced.) Participants could talk about textbooks and curricula available through the public schools, who reviews, purchases and dispenses curricula, why and how homeschoolers choose certain curricula, school district policies regarding home educators, state laws affecting school districts and home-based educators, and finally, how to open up and galvanize the home school/public school relationship.

To better inform community members about ever changing educational trends, issues and choices, additional public discussions could deal with the following:

- the privatization of public schools,
- the burgeoning charter school movement,
- alternative and magnet schools,
- vouchers and school choice,
- the separation of church and state,
- Internet and technology-based learning in the public schools,
- technology's role in reforming education,
- the current state of school/media centers,
- proposed school media center/public library mergers,
- the positive and negative sides of home education,
- the positive and negative sides of public schooling,
- children's educational rights,
- the new roles of parents and teachers in public education,

- state education agency mandates,
- the funding of public school districts,
- virtual schools and the future of education.

Participating as leaders and/or moderators in these public discussions, community-minded librarians could hone their facilitating skills, as well as learn about school curricula, educational options and many other subjects. These diverse programs would also be relevant for reference librarians; they could learn about current issues and gather up-to-date printed materials distributed at the discussions. These could eventually be added to the education and/or homeschooling resource files at the library.

This chapter has dealt with the library as homeschool laboratory, cooperation between librarians, home educators, and public school officials, the beginning of online homeschooling, technological changes, the future, homeschool/public school collaboration, and a variety of related subjects. Past chapters in this book have focused on homeschooling statistics, trends, educational styles, library outreach ideas, and real-life concerns and experiences. In the next narrative section I will review and condense the key ideas from these four chapters. My optimistic point of view is prevalent within these many pages and in this wrap-up. I believe there are an unlimited number of ways we can reach out to, and work with homeschoolers in our libraries.

Alice is stepping through the looking glass

Reaching an effective, high quality level of service to homeschoolers in our libraries is hard work, similar to farming. You need to remove the big field stones and trees before you plow the earth. (Remember to keep the stones piled in the corner of the field, a constant reminder of your hard work.) Once the field is cultivated, it's time to plant. Use all the land you have. Keep trying new seeds until you get it right. Experiment with companion planting. Regularly add nutrients to the soil. Aim for an inexpensive product you will be eager to share, and others may be willing to copy. Harvest the bounty.

Before we initiate services for homeschoolers we need to remove obstacles, such as stubborn mindsets, financial limitations, misapprehensions. Once over that hurdle, we need to understand that some obstacles never go away. The next step is to tap into the regional network of homeschoolers. Reach out and welcome them in for a library tour. Read and learn more about homeschooling. Seek to understand the diversity. Let homeschoolers know your intentions, ideas and boundaries. Plant honesty, not ambiguity. Some of your concepts will eventually take root. Listen to their beliefs and concerns. Encourage families to volunteer their time. Be flexible with your policies. Create a homeschooling resource file. If you have time and money, experiment with programs, classes, reading clubs, new resources and lots of technology. If these experiments work, share your success with other librarians, the library board of trustees, homeschoolers and public school teachers. Don't expect a utopia. Finally, give yourself a pat on the back and check the pile of obstacles!

When beginning your work and/or when making a decision whether to bother or not, try to keep the following summations of previous chapters in mind. All things considered, homeschooling is not a hot trend about to disappear. According to statistics from the past ten years, the number of homeschoolers is steadily growing. Many people agree the growth will eventually hit a ceiling where it will stop or level off. According to various researchers, currently about one percent of the school age children in this country are being taught at home; because of the possible impact and growth of technology-based homeschooling and numerous other factors, I believe that number may increase

to around four to five percent. Since some home educators need not declare their intentions, most statistics are estimates based on assumptions, not absolutes.

Many parents who choose homeschooling have religious motivations, but it's impossible to stereotype or categorize home educators. Their educational styles are also very diverse. In recent years, with the advent of home computers and online services, people have begun to experiment with electronic curricula for their children. Telecomputing technology and CD-ROMs may dramatically influence who chooses to homeschool.

Tapping into the huge community of homeschoolers is no small task, but there are a number of time-tested methods that usually work. Some libraries have even created task forces to study library service options. Once you've made the connection, explain the features of your thorough homeschool resource file. Show how it helps librarians find answers to reference questions, and provides parents with a consistent source of current home education information. There are abundant opportunities for serving homeschoolers. Focus on three or four ways you can help and/or work alongside homeschoolers; you may want to provide certain reference or curriculum materials, offer children's programming or book discussion groups, give orientation/ reference and technology tours, provide Internet access, or a number of other cost effective services. (Accomplish this without ostracizing other library customers. Create and/or choose practical, cost efficient programs and other services that appeal to and benefit homeschoolers *and* other library customers.) Also, in my opinion it sometimes helps to recognize someone on the library staff as the homeschool liaison. This person deals with homeschooler concerns, programs, test proctoring, collection development questions, ILL requests and more. Besides, having a specific person at the library to talk with is comforting to homeschoolers.

Because of the increased popularity of home education, both as a partial supplement or replacement for traditional schooling, more homeschoolers will be utilizing libraries and their varied menu of services. Libraries will become home-school laboratories. Observation, research and technology experimentation will take place there. Librarians are naturally curious and concerned about a number of issues relating to home educators, including requests for reconsideration, reluctance to substitute curriculum materials, interlibrary loan usage, subject area depletion, and challenges with intent to censor. Although some librarians have had negative experiences with home educators, I feel that is more the exception than the norm. The potential for further collaboration between librarians and homeschoolers is likely and highly recommended. Both parties stand to learn and gain.

Libraries should strive to become free community learning centers, and librarians should assume community leadership roles, facilitating in-house classes and conferences for homeschoolers and other educators. Forging future partnerships between home educators, public school media center librarians/teachers/officials, and public librarians is also important. A primary, shared goal should be "awareness and cooperative use of community resources." Tensions between home-schoolers and public school administrators, and open disagreements between school districts and state departments of education are still festering, but seem to be starting to heal. Examples of successful home school/public school cooperation and open door policies are increasing. Continued collaboration looks promising.

In the present we are experiencing the future. Impossibilities are becoming realities. Alice has stepped through the looking glass—on the other side of the mirror, the radical future blossoms. We are witnessing the exciting start of a progressive synthesis of technologies. The semiconductor and fiber optics technologies are converging. Rival telecommunications corporations are fighting for control of the traffic on the information superhighway. Virtual schools, libraries and electronic learning networks are proliferating. To thrive in this exciting and competitive climate, libraries and librarians need to adapt to these mind boggling changes. In order to attract home educators and other customers, libraries need to become technologically rich environments. In my opinion, library staff need to master new information age skills to stave off the competition and survive. If already highly trained, they need to start seeing themselves as information age pioneers.

Professor James Sweetland from the University of Wisconsin-Milwaukee School of Library and Information Science envisions at least nine possible futures for public libraries. Ultimately, they all relate to "survival of the technological fittest." Extinction is his worst case scenario. In one of the brighter library scenarios, the "People's Information Center," Sweetland's librarians are highly trained information handlers. He predicts, "In view of the proliferation and complexity of information technology most people need to rely on an intermediary. The public library staff become skilled not only in retrieving information, but in evaluating it—in essence expanding the role of 'reader's advisor.' Realizing the economies of scale and efficiencies of collective funding, taxpayers increase support for the library. The library becomes the local 'information node,' combining the functions of bookstore, cable company, Internet node, and traditional library."[17]

On the other side of the looking glass, many challenging questions arise! In the future, will your library be the community meeting place where customers come to connect with emerging technologies? Or, will it focus on people and materials, instead of machines? In what ways will your library serve homeschoolers? Will it be through electronic links, programs, classes, basic or unique services? Is it likely you or someone on your library staff will encourage communication and cooperation between a variety of educational stakeholders? Will the library profession evolve into a huge group of information age pioneers? In your library, will taking action to improve service for homeschoolers be a calculated risk, or a necessary catalyst for change?

Summary

Some of my main reasons for writing this book were: 1) to increase your awareness of homeschoolers and the homeschooling movement, 2) to show examples of sensible and thrifty services that have worked in other libraries, 3) to provide reproducible lists of high quality home education and related resources (these are located in the section following this chapter), and 4) to encourage you to prepare for the future by implementing some time tested services, and/or experimenting with fresh ideas of your own. Hopefully, my opinions and the real-life anecdotes sprinkled throughout these pages will inspire you to create a plan of action for serving homeschoolers. Good luck! I hope something new and exciting emerges.

Endnotes

1. Germantown Junior and Young Adult Advisory Committee, Summary of Discussions, April 9, 1994, "Envisioning Montgomery County (MD) Libraries: 2000."

2. Churbuck, David C. "The Ultimate School Choice: No School At All." *Forbes*, (October 11, 1993):145-150.

3. *Ibid.*

4. *Ibid.*, p.150.

5. Natale, Jo Anna. "Understanding Home Schooling." *American School Board Journal*, 178 (September 1992):26-29.

6. El-Amin, Joyce. "Home Schooling a Legitimate Alternative." *WEAC News & Views*, (September 1990):18.

7. Wilson, Stephanie. "Can We Clear the Air About Home Schooling?" *Instructor*, (January 1988):11.

8. Bishop, Celia. "Home Schooling Parent Support Groups In Kansas: A Naturalistic Inquiry Into Their Concerns And Functions," Kansas State University, Ph.D. dissertation, 1991.

9. Mirochnik, Denise A. and Walter G. McIntire. "Homeschooling: Issues for Administrators," College of Education, University of Maine, Occasional paper, May 1991.

10. Holt, John. "Schools And Home Schoolers: A Fruitful Partnership." *Phi Delta Kappan*, (February 1983):391-394.

11. Shepherd, Mike. "Home Schoolers As Public School Tutors." *Educational Leadership*, (September 1994):55-56.

12. Uzzell, Lawrence A. "Where Home-Schoolers Get a Helping Hand." *Wall Street Journal*, (November 27, 1990): 14.

13. Terpstra, Mary. "A Home School/School District Partnership." *Educational Leadership*, (September 1994):57-58.

14. Clark, Charles S. "Home Schooling: Is It a Healthy Alternative to Public Education?" *The CQ Researcher*, (September 9, 1994):787.

15. *Ibid.*

16. Ramsey, Krista. "Home Is Where the School Is." *The School Administrator*, (January 1992):25.

17. Sweetland, James H. "Possible Futures for Public Libraries," UW-Milwaukee, School of Library and Information Science, unpublished paper, 1995.

Appendix I

Homeschooling Organizations

National

Adventist Home Educator
P. O. Box 836
Camino, CA 95709

Alliance for Parental Involvement in Education
(ALLPIE)
P. O. Box 59
East Chatham, NY 12060
(518) 392-6900

Alternative Education Resource Organization
417 Roslyn Rd.
Roslyn Heights, NY 11577
(516) 621-2195

Association for Humanistic Education
P.O. Box 923
Carrolton, GA 30117

Christian Home Educators Association
(CHEA)
P. O. Box 2009
Norwalk, CA 90651-2009
(714) 537-5121

The Educational Association of Christian Homeschoolers (TEACH)
P.O. Box 91
Bloomfield, CT 06002

Fairtest, National Center for Fair and Open Testing
342 Broadway
Cambridge, MA 02139-1802
(617) 864-4810

Hewitt Research Foundation
P. O. Box 9
Washougal, WA 98671
(206) 348-1750

Holt Associates/Growing Without Schooling
2269 Massachusetts Avenue
Cambridge, MA 02140
(617) 864-3100

Home Education League of Parents (HELP)
3208 Cahuenga Blvd. West
Los Angeles, CA 90068
(800) 582-9061 or (213) 874-8007

Home School Legal Defense Association
P. O. Box 159
Paeonian Springs, VA 22129
(703) 338-5600
(The National Center for Home Education is also located at this address.)

Homeschooling Information Clearinghouse
P. O. Box 293023
Sacramento, CA 95829

Islamic Homeschool Association of North America
1312 Plymouth Ct.
Raleigh, NC 27610

Jewish Home Educator's Network
East Coast office
2 Webb Road
Sharon, MA 02067
(617) 784-9091

Jewish Home Educator's Network
West Coast office
P. O. Box 300
Benton City, WA 99320
(509) 588-5013

Latter Day Saints Home Educators Association
2770 South 1000 West
Perry, UT 84302
(801) 723-5355

The Moore Foundation
Box 1
Camas, WA 98607
(206) 835-2736

National Association of Catholic Home Educators (NACHE)
P.O. Box 420225
San Diego, CA 92142

National Challenged Homeschoolers Associated Network
5383 Alpine Road SE
Olalla, WA 98359
(206) 857-4257

National Association for the Legal Support of Alternative Schools
P. O. Box 2823
Santa Fe, NM 87501-2823
(505) 471-6928

National Coalition of Alternative Community Schools
P.O. Box 15036
Santa Fe, NM, 87506
(505) 474-4312

National Home Education Guild
515 North Eighth Street
Grants Pass, OR 97526
(503) 474-1501

National Home Education Research Institute
5000 Deer Park Dr. SE
Salem, OR 97301-7018
(503) 581-8600
Fax: (503) 585-4316

National Home Study Council
1601 18th. Street N.W.
Washington D. C. 20009
(202) 234-5100

National Homeschool Association
P. O. Box 157290
Cincinnati, OH 45215-7290
(513) 772-9580

Parents and Teachers for Social Responsibility
Box 517
Moretown, VT 05660
(802) 223-3409

Parents Association of Christian Schools
HC 63
Box 5530
Mayer, AZ 86333
(602) 632-7351

Single Parents Educating Children In Alternative Learning (SPECIAL)
2 Pineview Drive, #5
Amelia, OH 45102
(513) 753-0461

Unschoolers Network
2 Smith Street
Farmingdale, NJ 07727
(908) 938-2473

Military homeschool organizations

Christian Home Educators on Foreign Soil (CHEFS)
HHB V Corps Arty Unite 25212
APO AE 09079.

The Military Homeschooler (newsletter)
849 Leehigh Drive
Merced, CA 95348
European edition: HHC 160th Sig Bde
A.P.O., NY 09164

On the Move (newsletter)
1435 N.W. 9 Court
Homestead, FL 33030

Canadian Homeschool Organizations

Alberta Home Education Association
Box 3451
Leduc, AB
Canada T9E 6M2
(403) 986-4264

Canadian Alliance of Home Schoolers
195 Markville Rd.
Unionville
Ontario, L3R 4VB Canada
(416) 470-7930

Canadian Home Educators Association of British Columbia
4684 Darin Ct.
Kelowna, BC
Canada V1W 2B3
(604) 764-7462

Greater Vancouver Home Learners Support Group
Box 39009 Pt Grey RPO
Vancouver, BC
Canada V6R 4P1
(604) 228-1939

Home and Hearth
Box 1176
Bow Island, AB T0K 0G0
(403) 545-6021

Home Learning Resource Center
Box 61
Quathiaski, BC
Canada V0P 1NO

Homeschoolers Association of Alberta
8754 Connors Rd.
Edmonton, AB
Canada T5R 2V7

Manitoba Association for Schooling at Home
89 Edkar Cres
Winnipeg, MB
Canada R2G 3H8

Montreal Homeschoolers' Support Group
5241 Jacques Grenier
Montreal, PQ
Canada H3W 2G8
(514) 481-8435

Moore Canada
Box 500
Lillooet, BC V0K 1V0
(604) 256-7487
Fax: (604) 256-7299

Nova Scotia Christian Home-schooler's Association
RR1
Falmouth, NS
Canada B0P 1L0

Nova Scotia Homeschool Support Group
RR1
Pleasantville, NS
Canada B0R 1G0

Pinewood Alternative School
RR3
Millbrook, ON
Canada L0A 1GO (705) 932-3129

Quebec Home Schooling Advisory/Conseil pour l'Education a Domocile au Quebec
P.O. Box 1278
1002 Rosemarie Val David, Quebec
Canada J0T 2N0 (819) 322-6495

Saskatchewan Government Correspondence School
1855 Victoria Ave.
Regina, SK
Canada S4P 3V7
(306) 787-6024 or (800) 667-7166

International home education organizations

Christian Home Educators of the Caribbean
Palmas Del Mar Mail Service
Box 888
273 Humacao, PR 00791
(809) 852-5284

Christian Home Schoolers of New Zealand
4 Tawa St.
Palmerston North
New Zealand (06) 357-4399

Education Otherwise
P.O. Box 120
Leamington Spa
Warwickshire, CV32 7ER
England
(926) 886828

The Home Service
37 Balmoral Crescent
Dronfield Woodhouse
Sheffield, S18 5ZY
England

Homeschoolers Australia pty. ltd
P.O. Box 420
Kelleyville, NSW 2153 (02) 629-3927
Fax: (02) 629-3278

New Zealand Home Schooling Association
5 Thanet Ave.
Mt. Albert
Auckland 3
New Zealand

Intellectual freedom organizations

American Library Association Office for Intellectual Freedom
50 East Huron Street
Chicago, IL 60611
(312) 944-6780

National Coalition Against Censorship
275 Seventh Avenue
New York, NY 10001
(212) 807-6222

People for the American Way
2000 M St. NW
Suite 400, Washington, DC 20036
(202) 467-4999

Appendix II

Homeschooling Periodicals, Newspapers & Newsletters

National

Aero-Gramme
417 Roslyn Road
Roslyn Heights, NY 11577
(516) 621-2195
Fax: (516) 625-3257

This is the Alternative Education Resource Organization newsletter.

The Christian Educator
502 W. Euclid Avenue
Arlington Heights, IL 60004
Published by the Christian Liberty Academy.

The Drinking Gourd
P. O. Box 2557
Redmond, WA 98073
(206) 836-0336

This is subtitled as the "Multicultural Home-Education Magazine." Annual subscription is $15.

Freebies Magazine
1135 Eugenia Place
Carpenteria, CA 93013

A practical and fun publication from the same company that supplies Freebies for Teachers, Freebies for Kids and Freebies for Families. A sample issue is $2.

Good Apple Newspaper
Box 299
Carthage, IL 62321-0299
(800) 435-7234

These are the publishers who produce all the Good Apple trade paperbacks. This newspaper and other publications are definitely worth investigating; toll free number is listed above. Annual subscription is $16.95.

Growing Without Schooling
Holt Associates, Inc.
2269 Massachusetts Avenue
Cambridge, MA 02140
(617) 864-3100

This is a popular periodical, founded in 1977 by John Holt. It includes many "real-life" examples of home education. Annual subscription is $25.

Holistic Education Review
P.O. Box 1476
Greenfield, MA 01302

Free sample copies are available; annual subscription is $26 for individuals, $40 for institutions.

Home Education Magazine
P.O. Box 1083
Tonasket, WA 98855
(509) 486-1351
e-mail address is Hegener@aol.com

This is a high quality, well-balanced homeschooling periodical. Annual subscription is $24.

Home-made Schooling
RR 1, Box 188
Atwood, IL 61913

This is a monthly home-published magazine, designed for Christian homeschoolers. Annual subscription is $15.

Home School Court Report
P.O. Box 159
Paeonian Springs, VA 22129
(703) 882-3838

This is a nationwide publication covering home education legal issues.

Home School Digest
P.O. Box 575
Winona Lake, IN 46590

You can sample this Christian homeschooling magazine for $2.00. Annual subscription is $15.

Home School Helper
Bob Jones University Press
Greenville, SC 29614
(800) 845-5731

This is a national Christian publication.

Home School Researcher
5000 Deer Park Drive S.E.
Salem, OR 97301-9392
(503) 581-8600

Published by the National Home Education Research Institute, this newsletter takes a scholarly approach to homeschooling. $25 annual subscription rate.

Homeschooling: The HOW TO Newsletter
10404 Hunstmoor Drive
Richmond, VA 23233.

An inexpensive, practical, brief Christian newsletter published by homeschooling author Gayle Graham. $1 per issue.

Homeschooling Freedoms At Risk, a 1991 reprint available from Home Education Magazine (address listed above), written by Mark and Helen Hegener, influential homeschool advocates.

Homeschooling Today: Practical Help for Christian Families
P.O. Box 1425
Melrose, FL 32666
(904) 462-7201
Annual subscription $16.

Kid/News
P.O. Box 292
Mt. Vernon, OH 43050
A publication produced by and for homeschooled kids. $12 annual subscription/sample $1.

Learning Edge
1289 Jewett St.
Ann Arbor, MI 48104

This publication is from the Clonlara School, a long established correspondence school; it is nationwide in scope and includes home education news and articles by homeschooled children.

Mentor
3208 Cahuenga Blvd. West, Suite 131
Los Angeles, CA 90068
(800) 582-9061

The monthly newsletter of the Home Education League of Parents (HELP), designed for all kinds of homeschoolers.

Montana Homeschool Reference Guide
P.O. Box 960
Seeley Lake, MT 59868
(406) 754-2481

My favorite home education publication--even though the emphasis is regional, this is an excellent, comprehensive annual newspaper that touches on statewide and national homeschooling issues. It always includes scores of current addresses, support groups and interesting advertisements, and unabashed opinions. Free samples are usually available, especially for libraries.

Moore Report International
Box 1
Camas, WA 98607
(206) 835-2736

Subscriptions are $12 annually, for six issues; this Christian newspaper is a publication created by Dr. Raymond S. Moore and his wife Dorothy Moore. They are seen by some people as the "grandparents of the homeschooling movement."

NATHHAN News
5383 Alpine Road SE
Olalla, WA 98359

A publication from the National Challenged Homeschoolers Associated Network.

Options In Learning
P.O. Box 59
East Chatham, NY 12060-0059
(518) 392-6900

A non-sectarian quarterly publication.

Parent Educator and Family Report
P.O. Box 9
Washougal, WA 987671-0009
(206) 348-1750

A bi-monthly Christian publication from the Hewitt Research Foundation, a well-respected child development and testing service center.

Pennsylvania Homeschoolers Magazine
R.D. 2, Box 117
Kittanning, PA 16201
(412) 783-6512

A very attractive and interesting periodical, designed for all homeschoolers.

Practical Homeschooling
P.O. Box 1250
Fenton, MO 63026-1850
Fax: (314) 225-0743

This is a fine quarterly publication from talented homeschooling mother and author Mary Pride. Annual subscription $15.

Prairie: A Bulletin on Parental Rights and Responsibilities in Education
2545 Koshkonong Road
Stoughton, WI 53589

This newsletter, coordinated by outspoken homeschooling author Larry Kaseman, is designed to empower people to make their own, informed decisions on home education issues. Subscription rate $20 annually.

Rethinking Schools
1001 E. Keefe Avenue
Milwaukee, WI 53212
(414) 964-9646

A quarterly publication (sent out only during the public school year) that examines and creates controversial issues regarding education. Typical articles may address rethinking curriculum, teaching about Christopher Columbus, the Gulf War, outcome based education, children's books on South Africa, standardized testing, parental involvement in education, teacher unions, critical thinking, charter schools and school reform. Write or call for bulk order prices; subscription price $12.50.

Scholastic Classroom Magazines
P.O. Box 3710
Jefferson City, MO 65102

This well-known educational publisher offers more than two dozen magazines on topics such as: math, language arts, science, Spanish & French, current news and art. Subscriptions vary; $5 minimum.

The Teaching Home
P.O. Box 20219
Portland, OR 97220-0219
(503) 253-9633
Fax: (503) 253-7345

A handsome, bi-monthly magazine designed to provide information and inspiration to Christian homeschooling families and organizations. Annual subscription $15.

TIDBITS
P.O. Box 2823
Santa Fe, NM, 87501-2823
(505) 471-6928

Published by the National Association for the Legal Support of Alternative Schools (NALSAS), this semi-annual newsletter provides a variety of non-sectarian home education information.

Umoja Unidad Unity
5621 S. Lakeshore Drive
Idlewild, MI 49642

A bi-monthly publication for homeschoolers of color; subscription rate $12.

Under the Apple Tree: Elementary Activities for the Creative At-home Educator
P.O. Box 8
Woodinville, WA 98072

A bi-monthly periodical full of practical, fun ideas and activities; subscription $18, with sample copy available for $3.

Weekly Reader
245 Long Hill Road
Middletown, CT 06457

Many full color periodicals are available from this popular publisher; they focus on a wide variety of topics, for different age and ability levels.

International

The Home Schooler
Pleasant Hills, NSW
Australia 2658
(060) 29 0167

A quarterly magazine for homeschoolers in the South Pacific region; subscription is $10. A New Zealand edition is also available.
Albany Heights Rd.
RD 2 Albany, New Zealand

The Learning Leaf
R.R. 1, site 24
Comp. 36
Winfield, B.C.
Canada V0H 2C0

A practical magazine of interest to public and home educators; $15 for 6 issues, or send $2 for informational packet and sample issue.

Moore Canada
Box 500, Lillooet
B.C., Canada V0K 1H0
(604) 256-7487

International Christian newsletter available for $25 annual fee.

Myrrh: A Newsletter for Christian Home Schooling Families
197-919C Albert Street
Regina, Sask.
Canada S4R 2P6
(306) 545-8017
Fax: (306) 569-8649

This publication has no subscription fees, but donations are accepted.

Natural Life
195 Markville Rd.
Unionville, Ontario
Canada L3R 4V8

This bi-monthly publication, edited by a well-known Canadian home educator, Wendy Priesnitz, focuses on different styles of homeschooling and related topics. The annual subscriptions are $21; other reference books related to home education in Canada are available through this publisher.

Quest, the Home Educator's Journal
1144 Byron Avenue
Ottawa, Ontario
Canada K2B 6T4
(800) 668-5878 (OK to dial from the U.S.)

A quarterly Christian periodical; subscriptions are $26.

Appendix III

Correspondence Schools and Instructional Service Providers

**A Beka Correspondence School/
A Beka Video Home School**
Box 18000
Pensacola, FL 32523-9160
(800) 874-2352

A Beka is allied with Pensacola Christian College; grades P-12 are covered.

ACE (Accelerated Christian Education) School of Tomorrow
P.O. Box 1438
Lewisville, TX 75067
(800) 925-7777

Classes using videos and/or computer software are available; P-12 grades offered.

Alaska Centralized Correspondence Study
Department of Education
P.O. Box GA
Juneau, AK 99811-0544
(907) 465-2835

Alpha Omega Publications
P.O. Box 3153
Tempe, AZ 85280
(800) 821-4443

K-12 materials are available through this company.

American School
850 E. 58th. Street
Chicago, IL 60637
(312) 947-3300

Only standard traditional high school curriculum is offered.

Brigham Young University
Department of Independent Study
206 Harman Continuing Education Building
Provo, UT 84602

Calvert School
Dept. 2hsm
105 Tuscany Road
Baltimore, MD 21210
(410) 243-6030
Fax: (410) 366-0674

Provides a wide variety of full lesson plans for K-8. This correspondence school has been around for nearly ninety years.

Christian Liberty Academy Satellite Schools
(CLASS)
502 W. Euclid Avenue
Arlington Heights, IL 60004
(708) 259-8736

This school has K-12 offerings with some textbooks available.

Clonlara School Home Based Education
1289 Jewett
Ann Arbor, MI 48104
(313) 769-4515

Founded and directed by Dr. Pat Montgomery, innovative educator (taught in public/parochial schools for 14 years) and independent learning advocate, Clonlara serves families in ten countries.

Country Garden School
P.O. Box 6
College Place, WA 99324
(509) 525-0125

Family Learning Services
1755 Graham Drive
Eugene, OR 97405
(503) 686-0851.

This school helps plan Christian educational alternatives.

Hewitt Research Foundation
P.O. Box 9
Washougal, WA 98671
(206) 348-1750

Certified teachers coordinate and supervise this K-12 program.

Home Study International
P.O. Box 4437
Silver Spring, MD 20914-4437
(301) 680-6570
Fax: (301) 680-6577

This program offers K-12 plus some university classes, with a Christian emphasis.

Keys to Learning International
1411 Oak St. So.
Pasadena, CA 91030
(818) 799-0787

This K-12 school uses an "open-ended lesson plan method."

Landmark
P.O. Box 849
Fillmore, CA 93016
(805) 524-2388

Materials are available for K-12; focus is on ability to research and reason.

Lindenwood Academy
P.O. Box 3405
Fort Smith, AR 72913
(501) 782-6277

Grades P-12 are covered; diploma issued upon completion of classes.

McGuffey Academy International
2213 Spur Trail
Grapevine, TX 76051
(817) 481-7008

This is a complete correspondence service.

The Moore Academy
Box 1
Camas, WA 98607
(206) 835-5500

K-12 grades are included; Christian home education based on Dr. Raymond Moore's ideas and a variety of materials.

Oak Meadow, Inc.
P.O. Box 712
Blacksburg, VA 24063
(703) 731-3263.

A K-12 correspondence school using the precepts of Rudolph Steiner and Waldorf inspired curricula; the development of body, mind and spirit is emphasized.

Pinewood School
112 Road D
Pine, CO 80470
(303) 670-8180

This school features an online computer service and individualized curriculum.

Seton Home Study School
1350 Progress Drive
Front Royal, VA 22630
(703) 636-99900

Offers a K-12 Catholic program of correspondence.

Summit Christian Academy
P.O. Box 802041
Dallas, TX 75380
(800) 362-9180

This K-12 school uses the Alpha Omega curriculum and presently enrolls about 1,000 students.

The Sycamore Tree
2179 Meyer Place
Costa Mesa, CA 92627
(714) 650-4466

A complete homeschool program is available. Credentialed teachers help students choose which direction to follow with their correspondence schooling/home education. They also offer a catalog of books, equipment and supplies.

Appendix IV

Homeschool Curriculum and Resource Suppliers & Publishers

Books, curriculum and supplies

A Beka
P.O. Box 18000
Pensacola, FL 32523-9160
(800) 874-7472

A Beka is a well-known Christian book publisher.

Alpha Omega Publications
P.O. Box 3153
Tempe, AZ 85281
(800) 622-3070

This company sells a variety of K-12 materials and resources.

American Home Academy
2770 S. 1000 W. St.
Perry, UT 84302
(801) 723-5355

This is a Latter Day Saints curriculum and resource provider.

At Home Publications
2826 Roselawn Avenue
Baltimore, MD 21214-1719.

Backyard Scientist
P.O. Box 16966
Irvine, CA 92713

Bluestocking Press
P.O. Box 1014, Dept. 6
Placerville, CA 95667-1014

Call (800) 959-8586 to place orders; their catalog of resources includes audiotapes, books, toys, books and historical documents.

Bob Jones University Press
Greenville, SC 29614

Call (800) 845-5731 to place orders for these Christian-based K-12 materials and/or curricula.

Chinaberry Book Service
2830 Via Orange Way, Suite B
Spring Valley, CA 92078-1521.

Christian Liberty Academy
502 Euclid Avenue
Arlington Heights, IL 60004
(312) 259-8736

CLA is a popular Christian school and supplier of resources/curriculum materials.

Cobblestone Publishing
7 School St.
Peterborough, NH 03458
(800) 821-0115

Cobblestone publishes excellent, slick magazines on U.S. history, different cultures and world history.

Creative Learning Systems, Inc.
16510 Via Esprillo
San Diego, CA 92127-1708
(800) 458-2880

Creative Teaching Materials
P.O. Box 7766
Fresno, CA 93747
Call (800) 767-4282, for free catalog

Critical Thinking Press
P.O. Box 448
Pacific Grove, CA 93950
(800) 458-4849

Deckard, Dr. Steve
228 Central Drive
Briarcliff Manor, NY 10510
(914) 923-0838

Deckard is the author of *Home Schooling Laws in All Fifty States*; he distributes other home education materials also.

Delta Education Inc.
P.O. Box 950
Hudson, NH 03051
(800) 442-5444

This company features hands-on math and science projects; free catalog.

Design-A-Study
408 Victorian Avenue
Wilmington, DE 19804-2124
(302) 998-3889

Christian educator and homeschooler Kathryn Stout's company, featuring practical resources for home study.

Edmund Scientific Company
101 E. Gloucester Pike
Barrington, NJ 08007-1380
(609) 547-8880

Send for a free catalog of games/projects.

Educational Insights
19560 South Rancho Way
Dominguez Hills, CA 90220
(800) 995-4436

A free catalog is available.

Educational Products Group
Corporate Support Bldg., Suite 336
1000 Centerville Turnpike
Virginia Beach, VA 23463
(804) 523-7950.

Educators Publishing, Inc.
75 Moulton Street
Cambridge, MA 02138-1104
Call (800) 225-5750 for a free K-12 secular materials catalog.

The Elijah Co.
P.O. Box 12483
Knoxville, TN 37912-0483
(615) 475-7500

Send for a free catalog/home school manual from this supplier.

Family Learning Center
Route 2, Box 264
Hawthorne, FL 32640
(904) 475-5869

A distributor of educational products covering many topics.

Farm Country General Store
Rt. 1 Box 63
Metamora, IL 61548

Call (800) 551-FARM, for curriculum, kits and free catalog.

Fearon Teacher Aids
Box 280
Carthage, IL 62321

This major publisher offers a variety of publications appropriate for home educators.

Gayle Graham
10404 Hunstmoor Drive
Richmond, VA 23233
(804) 741-5650
Fax: (804) 741-1024

Author of the *How to Home School Newsletter*, acting as a clearinghouse for home education supplies.

Geode Educational Options
P.O. Box 106
West Chester, PA 19381-0106

For $2 you can obtain a catalog with resources that foster ecological and ethical lifestyles, teaching and parenting.

Great Christian Books Catalog
229 S. Bridge Street
P.O. Box 8000
Elkton, MD 21922-8000.

Hewitt Research Foundation
P.O. Box 9
Washougal, WA 98671

Highsmith Inc.
P.O. Box 800
Ft. Atkinson, WI 53538-0800
(800) 558-2110

Offers a free catalog containing a good variety of school and library supplies and resources.

Home Education Press
P.O. Box 1083
Tonasket, WA 98855
(509) 486-1351

An excellent, informative catalog, full of good home education books.

Home School Supply House: Learning Materials for All Ages
P.O. Box 7
Fountain Green, UT 84632
(800) 772-3129

A comprehensive catalog, including Dover books, classic home education titles, and more.

John Holt's Book & Music Store
2269 Massachusetts Avenue
Cambridge, MA 02140
(617) 864-3100
Fax: (617) 864-9235

Holt Associates supplies all John Holt books, homeschooling T-shirts, textbooks and other curriculum supplies, John Gatto videotapes, and tapesets.

KidsArt
P.O. Box 274
Mt. Shasta, CA 96067
(916) 926-5076

This publisher offers a great magazine, and arts/crafts books.

KONOS
P.O. Box 1534
Richardson, TX 75083
(214) 669-8337

Call for a free catalog from this Christian curriculum and resource supplier.

Math Products Plus
P.O. Box 64
San Carlos, CA 94070
(415) 593-2839

The Moore Foundation
Box 1
Camas, WA 98607
(206) 835-2736

Mortensen Math
P.O. Box 98
Hayden, ID 83835-0098
(208) 667-1580

Mott Media
1000 E. Huron Street
Milford, MI 48042
(800) 348-6688

McGuffy Readers and other classic books are available from this source.

Music for Little People
Box 1460
Redway, CA 95560
(800) 346-4445

Their free catalog features multi-cultural music for people of all ages.

Quality Educational Resources
P.O. Box 847
Cupertino, CA 95015-0847
(408) 252-2254

A free materials catalog is available.

The Riggs Institute
4185 S.W. 102nd Avenue
Beaverton, OR 97005
(503) 646-9459
Fax: (503) 644-5191

This supplier offers an instructional materials catalog that includes: phonics, writing and spelling curriculum, video seminars and lessons on many other topics

Riverside Schoolhouse
HCR 34 Box 181A
Bemidji, MN 56601

This company focuses on the popular Usborne books.

Rod & Staff Publishers
Highway 172
Crockett, KY 41413
(606) 522-4348

A Christian supply house; free catalogs and sample periodicals are available.

Saxon Publishers, Inc.
1320 West Lindsey
Norman, OK 73069
(405) 329-7071

Saxon produces and distributes K-12 mathematics products for home educators--including some for calculus and physics.

Scientific Wizardry Educational Products
9925 Fairview Avenue
Boise, ID 83704
(208) 377-8575

Sing and Learn Curriculum Supplies
2626 Club Meadow
Garland, TX 75043
(214) 840-8342

SyberVision
One Sansome Street, Suite 1610
San Francisco, CA 94104
(800) 888-9885

This is a good source for foreign language materials.

The Sycamore Tree
2179 Meyer Place
Costa Mesa, CA 92627

They offer a full range of books, computer software, audio and videotapes, educational games, supplies and kits.

Timberdoodle Company
E 1510 Spencer Lake Road
Shelton, WA 98584
(206) 426-0672

This Christian supplier carries Bible resources, maps and puzzles, resource books, curriculum materials and flashcards.

TOPS Learning Systems
10970 S. Mulino Road
Canby, OR 97013
Fax (503) 266-5200

TOPS distributes a free catalog to educators twice yearly.

Weaver Curriculum Series
2752 Scarborough
Riverside, CA 92503
(714) 688-3126

Word Publishers
4800 W. Waco Drive
Waco, TX 76796
(817) 772-7650

Many home education books are published by this Christian publisher.

World Book International
Educational Services Department
Northwest Point Blvd.
Elk Grove Village, IL 60007

Many homeschoolers rely on World Book's *Typical Course of Study K-12* curriculum outline.

Young Masters Home-Study Tutorial Art Program
Gordon School of Art
2316 Oakwood Avenue
Green Bay, WI 54301

A formal visual arts training program for youngsters is offered through this program.

Zephyr Press
3316 North Chapel Avenue
P.O. Box 13448-E
Tucson, AZ 85732-3448
(602) 322-5090

A good source for architectural supplies, art appreciation and math games.

Zondervan Publishing Co.
1415 Lake Drive S.E.
Grand Rapids, MI 49506
(800) 253-4475

This large publisher supplies Bible study sets, etc.

Appendix V

Suppliers of Home Education Video and Audiotapes

Christian Liberty Academy
502 Euclid Avenue
Arlington Heights, IL 60004
(312) 259-8736

Holt Associates, Inc.
2219 Massachusetts Avenue
Cambridge, MA 02140
(617) 864-3100

Home Life
P.O. Box 1250
Fenton, MO 63026
Mary Pride's supply house.

Home School Legal Defense Association
P.O. Box 159
Paeonian Springs, VA 22129
(703) 338-5600

International Linguistics
3505 E. Red Bridge Road
Kansas City, MO 64137
(800) 237-1830 or (816) 765-8855

KONOS
P.O. Box 1534
Richardson, TX 75083
(214) 669-8337

Moore Foundation
Box 1
Camas, WA 98067
(208) 835-2736

Used curriculum suppliers

The Book Cellar
87 Union Square
Milford, NH 06055
(800) 338-4257

The Home School Shopper
P.O. Box 11041
Spring Hill, FL 34610
(813) 856-5160

Mustard Seed Educational Services
120 Winston Section Rd.
Winston, OR 97496
(503) 679-3218

Titus Woman's Potpourri
10817 NE 45th St.
Kirkland, WA 98033
(206) 822-7337 or (800) 388-4887

Wilcox & Follett
1000 W. Washington Blvd.
Chicago, IL 60607

Appendix VI

Educational and/or Homeschooling Software Suppliers

Addison-Wesley
Route 128
Reading, MA 01867
(617) 944-3700

Advanced Ideas
2902 San Pablo Avenue
Berkeley, CA 94702
(415) 526-9100

American Education Corporation
7506 N. Broadway Ext., Suite 505
Oklahoma City, OK 73116-9016
(800) 222-2811

American Education Publishing
150 E. Wilson Bridge Rd., #145
Columbus, OH 43085-2328
(800) 542-7833

One popular product is the Brighter Child math series (book & disc) for $9.95.

Brøderbund Software
17 Paul Drive
San Rafael, CA 94903-2101
(800) 521-6263

A free catalog and newsletter is available from Brøderbund.

Critical Thinking Press
P.O. Box 448
Pacific Grove, CA 93950
(800) 458-4849

K-12 software

Data-Ware
5737 64th Street
Lubbock, TX 79424

This supplier carries IBM and compatible software.

Dayspring Northwest
P.O. Box 330
Hansville, WA 98346
(206) 638-2338 or (206) 638-2337

Educational Resources
1550 Executive Drive
Elgin, IL 60123
(800) 624-2926

Free catalogs are available upon request.

Excel-Ed
P.O. Box 380154
San Antonio, TX 78280

Write for current information; this educational data bank provides low cost computer programs.

Home Computer Market
P.O. Box 385377
Bloomington, MN 55438
(612) 844-0462

This supplier touts computer hardware and software in their catalog.

Intelligent Software, Inc.
9609 Cypress Avenue
Munster, IN 46321
(800) 521-4518
Fax: (219) 924-9208.

Progressive Results
160 Old State Road
Ballwin, MO 63021-5915
(800) 966-1737
Fax: (314) 394-2501

Home tutoring software is available.

Scholastic Software
730 Broadway
New York, NY 10030
(212) 505-3561

Skills Bank
Home Tutor Edition
15 Governor's Court
Baltimore, MD 21244
(800) 42-TUTOR

Smartek Software
2223 Avenida De La Playa, Suite 108
La Jolla, CA 92037
(800) 858-WORD

Springboard Software
7808 Creekbridge Circle
Minneapolis, MN 55435
(612) 944-3915

Tandy Corp.
1500 One Tandy Center
Fort Worth, TX 76102
(817) 878-4969

Note: For extensive, annotated information on homeschooling software, consult the 608-page book entitled, *Pride's Guide to Educational Software,* by Mary and Bill Pride, available from Crossway Books, Wheaton, Illinois.

Appendix VII

Online Home Education Connections

Internet Usenet Newsgroups:

1. misc.education.home-school.christian
2. misc.education.home-school.misc

World Wide Web:

1. URL: http://www.armory.com/-jon/hs/ Homeschool.html

   This provides access to many homeschooling articles and mailing lists.

Bulletin Board Systems (BBS):

1. HUG BBS The Home Education Computer User's Group Bulletin Board. For further information, contact Jim Mayor, 26824 Howard Chapel Drive, Damascus, MD 20872.

2. ECCLESIA BBS
   (510) 526-6584 Berkeley, CA

3. SERVANT BBS
   (310) 371-2770 Redondo Beach, CA

4. GENTLE RAIN BBS
   (909) 593-6144 Claremont, CA

5. MAC'S LAST STAND
   (716) 247-9056 Rochester, NY

6. PENTECOM BBS
   (514) 425-4001 Montreal, Quebec

Appendix VIII

Homeschooling Bibliography

Articles and books written by and for librarians

Avner, Jane A. "Home Schoolers: A Forgotten Clientele?" *School Library Journal*, (July 1989): 29-33.

Gemmer, Theresa. "Homeschoolers and the Public Library." *ALKI*, (December 1987): 96-98.

Gemmer, Theresa. "The Library Response to Homeschooling." *ALKI*, (March 1991): 20-23.

Klipsch, Pamela R. "An Educated Collection for Homeschoolers." *Library Journal*, (February 1, 1995): 47-50.

LaRue, James and Suzanne LaRue. "Is Anybody Home? Schooling and the Library." *Wilson Library Bulletin*, (September 1991): 32-37.

Madden, Susan. "Learning At Home: Public Library Service to Homeschoolers." *School Library Journal,* (July 1991): 23-25.

Public Library Association, Parents Education Services Committee. "The Librarian's Home Education Resource Guide." Four-page handout, March 1991.

Scheps, Susan, ed. *Homeschoolers and the Public Library: A Resource Guide for Libraries Serving Homeschoolers*. Chicago: Public Library Association, 1993.

Informational articles on home education

Amsden, Diana Avery. "Two Generations of Home Schooling." *Mother Earth News*, (Nov/Dec 1980): 46-47.

Bruder, Isabelle. "Bringing It Home: Technology Could Change the Face of Home Learning." *Electronic Learning*, (April 1993): 20-21.

Churbuck, David C. "The Ultimate School Choice: No School At All." *Forbes,* (October 11, 1993):144-150.

Clark, Charles S. "Home Schooling: Is It a Healthy Alternative to Public Education?" *The CQ Researcher*, (September 9, 1994): 769-792.

Country Journal editors. "Lessons from Home: A Special Section." *Country Journal*, (January/February 1994): 37-51.

Guterson, David. "When Schools Fail: An English Teacher Educates His Kids At Home." *Harper's*, (November 1990): 58-64.

Hancock, LynNell and Rob French. "The Dawn of Online Home Schooling." *Newsweek*, (October 10, 1994): 67.

Holt, John. "Schools and Home Schoolers: A Fruitful Partnership." *PHI DELTA KAPPAN*, (February 1983): 391-394.

Kaminski, Andrea. "Learning It At Home." *ISTHMUS*, (November 6, 1992):1 (5).

Kantrowitz, Barbara and Debra Rosenberg. "In a Class of Their Own." *Newsweek,* (January 10, 1994): 58.

Lamb, Lynette. "Do-it-yourself Schools: Many Parents are Now Teaching Their Kids at Home." *Utne Reader,* (March/April 1990): 32-33.

Leslie, Connie. "This Isn't PS 123: Public Funds for Home Schoolers?" *Newsweek,* (September 26, 1994): 70.

Miner, Barbara. "Home-Schoolers' Charter Under Attack." *Rethinking Schools,* (Autumn 1994): 20.

Moore, Raymond. "Homegrown and Home-schooled." *Mothering,* (Summer 1990): 79-83.

Natale, Jo Anna. "Understanding Home Schooling." *American School Board Journal,* (September 1992): 26-29.

Pike, Bob. "Why I Teach My Children at Home." *PHI DELTA KAPPAN,* (March 1992): 564-565.

Pride, Mary. "Highly Recommended Home-schooling Resources." *Whole Earth Review,* (Fall 1989): 124-131.

Ramsey, Krista. "Home Is Where the School Is: School Leaders Seek Ways to Keep Doors Open to Parents." *The School Administrator,* (January 1992): 20-25.

Rupp, Rebecca. "Teach Your Children Well." *Harrowsmith Country Life,* (September/October 1993): 26-35.

Seuffert, Virginia. "Home Remedy: A Mom's Prescription for Ailing Schools." *Policy Review,* (Spring 1990): 70-75.

Shepherd, Michael S. "Homeschooling: A Legal View." *Mothering,* (Spring 1988): 82-86.

Shepherd, Mike. "Home Schoolers as Public School Tutors." *Educational Leadership,* (September 1994): 55-56.

Smith D. S. "Home Schooling." *Mother Earth News,* (August/September 1993): 53 (3).

Stecklow, Steve. "Fed Up with Schools, More Parents Turn to Teaching at Home." *Wall Street Journal,* (May 10, 1994): A1 (2).

Terpstra, Mary. "A Home School/School District Partnership." *Educational Leadership,* (September 1994): 57-58.

Uzzell, Lawrence. "Where Home-Schoolers Get a Helping Hand." *Wall Street Journal,* (November 27, 1990): A16.

Wilson, Stephanie. "Can We Clear the Air about Home Schooling?" *Instructor,* (January 1988): 11.

Scholarly articles on home education

Knowles, J. G. "The Context of Homeschooling in the United States." *Education and Urban Society* 21, (1988): 5-15.

Knowles, J. G. "Cooperating with Home School Parents: A New Agenda for Public Schools?" *Urban Education* 23, (1989): 392-411.

Knowles, J. G. "From Pedagogy to Ideology: Origins and Phases of Home Education in the United States, 1970-1990." *American Journal of Education,* (February 1992): 195 (41).

Knowles, J. G. "Parents' Rationales for Home Education." *Journal of Contemporary Ethnography,* (July 1991): 203-230.

Lines, Patricia M. "An Overview of Home Instruction." *PHI DELTA KAPPAN* 68, (1987): 510-517.

Lines, Patricia M. "States Should Help, Not Hinder, Parents' Home-Schooling Efforts." *Education Week,* (May 15, 1985): 24.

Litcher, John H. and Steven J. Schmidt. "Social Studies in the Home School." *Social Education,* (April/May 1991): 239-241.

Mayberry, M. "Characteristics and Attitudes of Families Who Home School." *Education and Urban Society* 21, (1988): 32-41.

Montgomery, L. "The Effect of Home Schooling on the Leadership Skills of Home Schooled Students." *Home School Researcher* Vol. 5, (1989): 1-10.

Ray, B. D. "Home Schools: A Synthesis of Research Characteristics and Learner Outcomes." *Education and Urban Society* 21, (1988): 16-31.

Roach, V. "Home Schooling in Times of Educational Reform." *Education Digest* 54, (February 1989): 58-61.

Webb, J., "The Outcomes of Home-based Education: Employment and Other Issues." *Educational Review,* (1989): 41-42.

How-to books on homeschooling

Ballman, Ray. *The How and Why of Home Schooling*. Wheaton, Ill.: Crossway, 1987.

Barker, Britt. *Letters Home*. Tonasket, Wash.: Home Education Press, 1990.

Beechik, Ruth. *You Can Teach Your Child Successfully: The Three R's*. Pollock Pines, Calif.: Arrow Press, 1992.

Brooks, Bearl. *Home School Workbooks* (Grades 1-5). Largo, Fla.:ESP, 1983.

Castaneda, Deborah and Pam Geib. *Help, I'm Homeschooling*. Norwalk: CHEA, 1990.

Colfax, David and Micki. *Homeschooling for Excellence*. New York: Warner, 1988.

Dobson, Linda. *Reclaiming Your Family, Community and Self: The Wisdom of Family-Centered Learning*. Tonasket, Wash.: Home Education Press, 1994.

Duffy, Cathy. *Christian Home Educators' Curriculum Manual, Elementary Grades*. Garden Grove, Calif.: Home Run Enterprises, 1992.

Duffy, Cathy. *Christian Home Educators' Curriculum Manual, Junior/Senior High*. Garden Grove, Calif.: Home Run Enterprises, 1992.

Fugate, J. Richard. *Successful Home Schooling*. Tempe, Ariz.: Alpha Omega Publications, 1990.

Gelner, Judy. *College Admissions: A Guide for Homeschoolers*. Sedalia: Poppyseed Press, 1990.

Gorder, Cheryl. *Home Schools: An Alternative*. Tempe, Ariz.: Blue Bird Publishing, 1990.

Graham, Gayle. *How to Home School: A Practical Approach*. Richmond: Common Sense Press.

Guterson, David. *Family Matters: Why Homeschooling Makes Sense*. New York: Harcourt, Brace, Jovanovich, 1992.

Harris, Gregg. *Home Schooling Workshop*. Gresham: Noble Publishing Associates, 1988.

Hegener, Mark and Helen. *Homeschool Handbook*. Tonasket, Wash.: Home Education Press, 1994.

Hegener, Mark and Helen. *The Home School Reader: Perspectives on Home Schooling*. Tonasket, Wash.: Home Education Press, 1988.

Hendrickson, Borg. *Home Schooling: Taking the First Step*. Wrangell, Alaska: Mountain Meadow Press, 1989.

Hendrickson, Borg. *How to Write a Low Cost/No Cost Curriculum for Your Home-School Child*. Wrangell, Alaska: Mountain Meadow Press, 1990.

Holt, John. *Learning All the Time*. New York: Addison Wesley, 1989.

Holt, John. *Teach Your Own: A Hopeful Path for Education*. New York: Delacorte, 1982.

Hood, Mary. *The Relaxed Home School: A Family Production*. Tempe, Ariz.: Ambleside Educational Press, 1994.

Hubbs, Don. *Home Education Resource Guide*. Tempe, Ariz.: Blue Bird Publishing, 1994.

Kaseman, Larry and Susan. *Taking Charge Through Home Schooling: Personal and Political Empowerment*. Stoughton, Wis.: Koshkonong Press, 1991.

Llewellyn, Grace. *Real Lives: Eleven Teenagers Who Don't Go to School*. Eugene, Oreg.: Lowry House, 1993.

Llewellyn, Grace. *The Teenage Liberation Handbook*. Eugene, Oreg.: Lowry House, 1991.

Lopez. Diane. *Teaching Children: A Curriculum Guide to What Children Need to Know at Each Level Through Sixth Grade*. Wheaton, Ill.: Good News, 1988.

Moore, Raymond and Dorothy. *Home-Grown Kids*. Waco, Tex.: Word, 1981.

Moore, Dorothy and Raymond. *The Successful Homeschool Family Handbook: A Creative and Stress Free Approach to Homeschooling*. Nashville, Tenn.: Nelson, 1994.

O'Leary, Jennifer. *Write Your Own Curriculum*. Stevens Point, Wis.: Whole Life Publishing Co., 1993.

Pedersen, Anne and Peggy O'Mara. *Schooling At Home: Parents, Kids and Learning*. Sante Fe, N.M.: John Muir Publications, 1990.

Pride, Mary. *The Big Book of Home Learning* (5 volumes). Wheaton, Ill.: Crossway Books, 1991.

Pride, Mary. Schoolproof: *How to Help Your Family Beat the System and Learn to Love*

Learning—the Easy, Natural Way. Wheaton, Ill: Crossway Books, 1988.

Reed, Donn. *The Home School Source Book*. Bridgewater, Maine: Brook Farm Books, 1994.

Richman, Howard and Susan. *The Three R's at Home*. Kittaning: Pennsylvania Homeschoolers, 1988.

Richman, Susan. *Writing from Home: A Portfolio of Homeschooled Student Writing*. Kittaning: Pennsylvania Homeschoolers, 1990.

Riley, Dan. *The Dan Riley School for a Girl: An Adventure in Home Schooling*. New York: Houghton Mifflin, 1994.

Shackelford, Luanne and Susan White. *A Survivor's Guide to Home Schooling*. Wheaton, Ill.: Crossway Books, 1989.

Story Time Staff. *Homeschooling with Educational Story Rhymes*. Birmingham, Ala.: Story Time Publishing, 1993.

Wade, Theodore. *The Home School Manual: Plans, Pointers, Reasons and Resources*. Niles, Ill.: Gazelle Publications, 1994.

Wallace, Nancy. *Taking Children's Choices Seriously*. Cambridge, Mass.: Holt Associates, 1990.

Welch, Sue. *Home School Information*. Portland, Oreg.: Teaching Home, 1994.

Home education reference and resource books

Deckard, Steve W. *Homeschooling Laws In All Fifty States: State by State Home School Manual*. Santee: Steve Deckard, 1994.

Green, Diana Huss. *Parent's Choice: A Sourcebook of the Very Best Products to Educate, Inform, and Entertain Children of All Ages*. New York: Andrews & McMeel, 1993.

Hood, Mary. *The Home-Schooling Resource Guide and Directory of Organizations*. Tempe, Ariz.: Ambleside Educational Press, 1993.

Klicka, Christopher J. *The Right Choice: Home Schooling*. Gresham, Oreg.: Noble Publishing Associates, 1992.

Mintz, Jerry; editor. *The Handbook of Alternative Education*. New York: Macmillan, 1994.

Perelman, Lewis J. *School's Out: Hyperlearning, the New Technology, and the End of Education*. New York: William Morrow & Co., 1992.

Pride, Mary and Bill. *Pride's Guide to Educational Software*. Wheaton, Ill.: Crossway Books, 1992.

Ray, Brian D. *Home Education in Montana: Family Characteristics and Student Achievement*. Salem, Oreg.: National Home Education Research Institute, 1990.

Richman, Howard. *Story of a Bill: Legalizing Home Schooling in Pennsylvania*. Kittaning: Pennsylvania Homeschoolers, 1989.

Rupp, Rebecca. *Schooltools: Educational Resources for Parents and Teachers*. Tonasket, Wash.: Home Education Press, 1993.

Van Galen, Jane and Mary Anne Pitman; eds. *Home Schooling: Political, Historical, and Pedagogical Perspectives*. Norwood, N.J.: Ablex, 1991.

Whitehead, John W. and Alexis Irene Crow. *Home Education: Rights & Reasons*. Wheaton, Ill.: Crossway Books, 1993.

Williams, Jane A. *How to Stock a Home Library Inexpensively*. Placerville, Calif.: Bluestocking Press, 1995.

Wilson, Elizabeth L. *Books Children Love: A Guide to the Best Children's Literature*. Wheaton, Ill.: Crossway Books, 1987.

Appendix IX

A Homeschooling Survey for Librarians

1. Does your library work at identifying, reaching out, and actively serving homeschoolers?

2. Does your library have any special programs or services designed solely for homeschoolers?

3. Have you, or anyone in your library, experienced any problems with serving homeschoolers? For example, have there been any collection development challenges, ILL issues, censorship, curricula demands, or any other negative encounters? If so, please elaborate.

4. Please list some positive anecdotes concerning your personal experiences in serving home educators.

5. List public library programs you think would work with the homeschooling population.

6. How do you feel about providing curricula in your library for homeschoolers? What about extended loan periods and limits like public school teachers receive?

7. Any other overall comments on this topic? Where do you see homeschoolers making the biggest impact in your library, especially in the future?

Thanks for your comments!!

Index